ENGLISH in Common

2

with ActiveBook

Mark Foley and Diane Hall

Series Consultants
María Victoria Saumell and Sarah Louisa Birchley

ALWAYS LEARNING

PEARSON

ENGLISH in Common 2
with ActiveBook

Maria Victoria Saumell
Sarah Louisa Birchley

ALWAYS LEARNING PEARSON

English in Common is a six-level course that helps adult and young-adult English learners develop effective communication skills that correspond to the Common European Framework of Reference for Languages (CEFR). Every level of *English in Common* is correlated to a level of the CEFR, and each lesson is formulated around a specific CAN DO objective.

English in Common 2 has twelve units. Each unit has ten pages.

There are three two-page lessons in each unit.

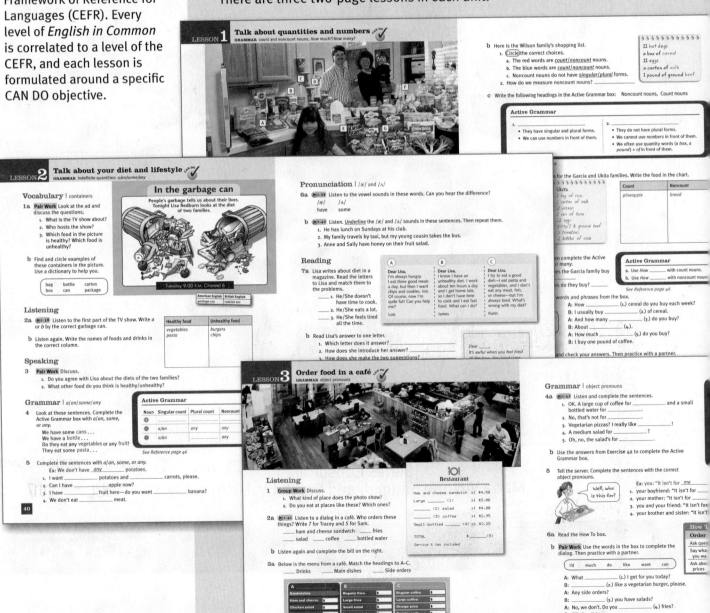

A two-page Unit Wrap Up and a Reference page end each unit.

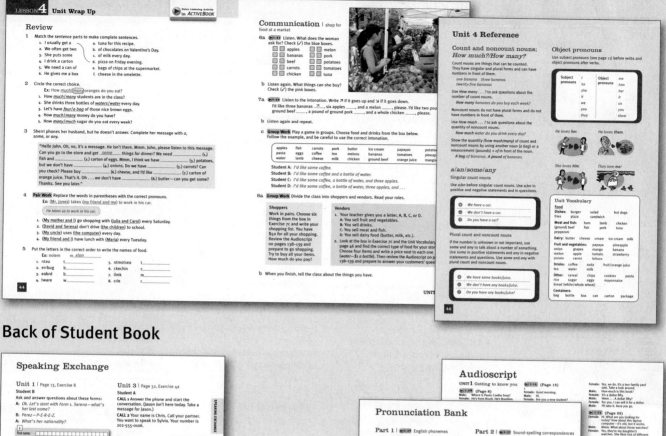

Back of Student Book

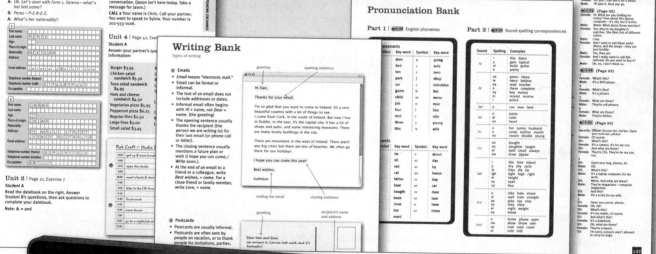

- Each Student Book contains an *ActiveBook*, which provides the Student Book in digital format. *ActiveBook* also includes the complete Audio Program and Extra Listening activities.

- An optional online **MyEnglishLab** provides the opportunity for extra practice anytime, anywhere.

- The Teacher's Resource Book contains teaching notes, photocopiable extension activities, and an *ActiveTeach*, which provides a digital Student Book enhanced by interactive whiteboard software. *ActiveTeach* also includes the videos and video activities, as well as the complete Test Bank.

Contents

UNIT	CAN DO OBJECTIVES	GRAMMAR	VOCABULARY/ EXPRESSIONS	
1 Getting to know you page 7	• talk about where you are from • exchange information about your family • understand and complete a simple form	• *be:* affirmative + subject pronouns • possessive *'s* • possessive adjectives • *yes/no* questions with *be* • articles: *a/an* • *be* negative + subject	• countries and nationalities • people and objects • families • jobs • beginning and ending a conversation	
2 Work and leisure page 17	• talk about your daily routine • write about a daily routine • identify everyday objects	• simple present: *I/you/we* • simple present: *he/she/it* • demonstratives: *this/that/these/ those* • plural nouns	• daily activities/routines • vacations • personal possessions • everyday objects	
3 Your free time page 27	• talk about your free time • talk about what you can and can't do • take and leave a simple phone message	• simple present: negative • *can/can't:* ability • *can:* requests • suggestions: *Let's/How about . . . ?/Why don't we . . . ?*	• activities • sports and games • making suggestions and requests	
4 Food page 37	• talk about quantities and numbers • talk about your diet and lifestyle • order food in a café	• nouns: count and non-count • quantities: *How much?/How many?* • indefinite quantities: *a/an/some/ any* • object pronouns	• food and drink • quantities • containers • ordering in a restaurant	
5 Around the house page 47	• talk about your home • talk about important possessions • write an informal email about your country	• *there is/there are:* statements and questions • *have/has:* possession and features • modifiers: *very/pretty/really*	• rooms • furniture • places • talking about where you live	
6 Around town page 57	• talk about your past • give and follow simple directions • describe your last vacation	• simple past of *be* • simple past: regular verbs	• places • prepositions of location • asking for and giving directions • transportation • asking where something is	
7 Describing people page 67	• write an informal letter describing family members • say who objects belong to • understand an article	• pronouns: *one/ones* • possessive pronouns • simple past: irregular verbs	• descriptive adjectives • starting and finishing an informal letter • ordinal numbers • months	
8 Dressing right page 77	• write a request to a colleague • describe what you are doing now • take part in a factual conversation	• adverbs: frequency and manner • present continuous • simple present and present continuous	• clothes • weather • giving your opinion and agreeing/disagreeing • making a complaint	
9 Entertainment page 87	• compare things • write a short film review • talk about personal preferences	• comparatives • superlatives • *like* + noun/gerund • *will:* spontaneous decisions/offers	• art forms • news media • movies • talking about preferences • discuss and plan activities	
10 Going places page 97	• talk about personal experiences • understand key points in a brochure • write a postcard • book a travel agent	• *be:* present perfect + *ever/never* • present perfect with regular and irregular verbs: *he/she/it* • gerund as subject	• methods of commuting • methods of travel • booking a ticket • reserving a hotel room • facilities and services	
11 Education page 107	• understand signs and rules • understand and produce a simple explanation • talk about future plans	• *can/can't:* permission: • *have to/don't have to:* obligation • review of *wh-* questions • future: present continuous	• education • school subjects • institutions • scheduling appointments	
12 Your goals page 117	• talk about intentions • write an informal letter • talk about likes/dislikes/goals	• *be going to* for intentions • infinitive of purpose • verb + infinitive/gerund	• geographical features • an informal letter • vigorous activities • descriptive adjectives: actions	

READING/WRITING	LISTENING	COMMUNICATION/ PRONUNCIATION
Reading texts: • a website • an employment form **Writing task:** fill in an employment form	**Listening tasks:** • determine relationships • perceive personal details • recognize greetings and expressions	**Communication:** start and finish a basic conversation **Pronunciation:** • stress • ʌ sound
Reading texts: • advertisements • articles about unusual jobs **Writing task:** complete a questionnaire	**Listening tasks:** • distinguish times • recognize key words • identify objects	**Communication:** ask questions for information and understand the answers **Pronunciation:** • verb endings • short and long vowel sounds
Reading texts: • an article about routines • an article about a famous athlete • an article about text messages **Writing task:** write a short article about your free time	**Listening tasks:** • discern specific words • recognize situations • understand phone messages • identify sequence	**Communication:** talk about other people's abilities **Pronunciation:** • vowel clarity in *can* and *can't* • stress in numbers
Reading texts: • an article about food around the world • letters in a magazine **Writing task:** write an answer to a letter	**Listening tasks:** • recognize key information • discern details • identify speakers • determine prices	**Communication:** shop for food at a market **Pronunciation:** • distinguishing between /æ/ and /ʌ/ • intonation
Reading texts: • a real estate brochure • an email to a friend **Writing task:** write an email to a friend	**Listening tasks:** • recognize main ideas • distinguish key words • determine important details • identify locations • discern specific words	**Communication:** talk about furnishing an apartment **Pronunciation:** distinguishing between /æ/ and /ɑ/
Reading texts: • descriptions of buildings • an article about a missing man • an article about navigation **Writing task:** write a paragraph about a vacation	**Listening tasks:** • understand directions • distinguish places	**Communication:** understand a directory and ask for things in stores **Pronunciation:** simple past form: *-ed*
Reading texts: • a letter from a student • an article about litter **Writing task:** write about where you live/your family	**Listening tasks:** • identify people • recognize key words • understand gist • discern details	**Communication:** identify a person from a simple description **Pronunciation:** producing /θ/
Reading texts: • an advice column about what to wear • a web page about health **Writing task:** write a letter requesting advice	**Listening tasks:** • identify actions • distinguish agreement and disagreement • determine solutions	**Communication:** make a complaint in a store **Pronunciation:** sentence rhythm
Reading texts: • an article about news sources • a movie quiz • an article about an artist **Writing task:** write a short movie review	**Listening tasks:** • identify opinions • recognize art from descriptions • distinguish key words	**Communication:** discuss and plan activities **Pronunciation:** producing /ɚ/
Reading texts: • a travel brochure • an article about commuters **Writing task:** write a postcard	**Listening tasks:** • understand the gist • determine meaning from context • understand problems and solutions	**Communication:** understand basic hotel information, reserve a room **Pronunciation:** long and short vowels
Reading texts: • an article about traffic school • an article about an educational system • an email from a friend **Writing task:** explain your country's educational system	**Listening tasks:** • identify comparisons • distinguish situations • understand key information and make notes	**Communication:** make future plans and appointments **Pronunciation:** intonation for *wh-* questions
Reading texts: • an article about continents • an informal letter from a friend • a web page about travel **Writing task:** write an informal letter to a friend	**Listening tasks:** • identify main ideas • understand gist • recognize opinions	**Communication:** plan study objectives **Pronunciation:** word stress

How much do you know . . . ?

1a ▶1.02 Do you know the alphabet? Listen and repeat the alphabet.

**a b c d e f g h i j k l m
n o p q r s t u v w x y z**

b **Pair Work** Write six consonants and three vowels. Read them to your partner.

Consonants: _____   Vowels: _____

2a ▶1.03 Do you know numbers? Match the numbers to the words. Then listen, check, and repeat.

| 0 | 1 | 2 | 3 | 4 | 5 | 6 | 7 | 8 | 9 | 10 |

eight   five   four   oh/zero   nine   one   seven   six   ten   three   two

b ▶1.04 Complete the sequence with numbers from the box. Then listen, check, and repeat.

eighty   fifty   fourteen   nineteen   ninety   seventeen   seventy   sixteen   thirty   twenty-two

11 eleven	16 _____	21 twenty-one	60 sixty
12 twelve	17 _____	22 _____	70 _____
13 thirteen	18 eighteen	30 _____	80 _____
14 _____	19 _____	40 forty	90 _____
15 fifteen	20 twenty	50 _____	100 a hundred

3a Do you know classroom instructions? Match the instructions to the pictures.

Match.   Correct.   Read.   Complete.   Ask and answer.
Write.   Repeat.   Listen.   Look at page . . .   Check your answers.

b ▶1.05 Listen and check your answers.

4 Do you know English words? Write more words in the chart.

Food/Drink	bread,	Sports	tennis,
Family	mother,	Transportation	taxi,
Objects	pencil,	Color	red,

UNIT 1
Getting to know you

Warm Up

1a ▶1.06 Complete the dialogs. Use the words in the box. Then listen and check.

> My name's Hi What's your I'm It's meet

1. A: Hi. _____ Jana. _____ name?
   B: _____ , Jana. _____ Dominik.
2. A: _____ name, please?
   B: _____ Patricia Pérez.
3. A: Hello. _____ Dan Cooper.
   B: Hello. _____ Lisa Chen. Nice to _____ you.

b **Pair Work** Practice the dialogs with a partner.

Talk about where you are from

GRAMMAR *be*: affirmative + subject pronouns

CAN DO ✓

Vocabulary | countries and nationalities

1 Find the countries on the map.

_B_ United States of America
____ Australia ____ Brazil ____ Canada
____ China ____ Colombia ____ France
____ Germany ____ Japan ____ Korea
____ Italy ____ Spain ____ Vietnam
____ Mexico ____ Great Britain

2 ▶1.07 Listen and complete the chart.

Country	Nationality	Ending
Australia	1. _Australian_	-(i)an
Brazil	2. _____	
Canada	Canadian	
Colombia	Colombian	
Italy	3. _____	
4. _____	German	
Korea	Korean	
Mexico	5. _____	
United States of America	6. _____	
7. _____	Spanish	-ish
Great Britain	8. _____	
China	9. _____	-ese
Japan	Japanese	
Vietnam	Vietnamese	
10. _____	French	

3a **Pair Work** Look at the photos. Write the letter of the photo next to the name.

____ Penélope Cruz _a_ Paulo Coelho
____ Gael García Bernal ____ Andrea Bocelli
____ Helen Mirren ____ Gérard Depardieu
____ Hideki Matsui ____ Nicole Kidman
____ Ralf and Michael Schumacher ____ Gong Li
____ Will Smith and Jada Pinkett Smith

b ▶1.08 Listen to the dialog. Find out where each person is from. Write the country under the photo.

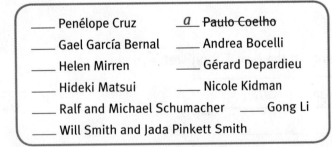

a _____ b _____ c _____
Brazil

d _____ e _____ f _____

g _____ h _____ i _____

j _____ k _____

Madrid•

Shenyang•

Pacific Ocean

Indian Ocean

4 **Pair Work** Ask and answer questions about the people in the photos.

> Where is Paulo Coelho from?

> He's from Brazil. He's Brazilian.

Pronunciation | stress

5a ▶1.09 Look at the chart in Exercise 2. Listen and repeat the nationality words.

b Listen again. <u>Underline</u> the stress in each word (*Austr<u>al</u>ian*).

c **Pair Work** Practice the words. **Student A:** Say a name. **Student B:** Say the nationality.

> Nicole Kidman

> She's Australian.

Grammar | *be* affirmative + subject pronouns

6a Complete the Active Grammar box with *am, is,* or *are.*

b **Pair Work** Complete the sentences. Then practice with a partner.

       Ex: I'_m__ Brazilian. __I__'m from São Paulo.

   1. Jennifer Lopez _____ American. _____'s from New York.

   2. We'_____ Korean. _____'re from Seoul.

   3. **A:** Excuse me, where _____ you _____ ?
      B: I'_____ from Colombia.

   4. **A:** What is _____ ? **B:** It'_____ a dictionary.

   5. **A:** Who are _____ ? **B:** They'_____ students in my class.

Active Grammar

I _____ (I'm)	
You _____ (you're)	
He _____ (he's)	
She _____ (she's)	from
It _____ (it's)	Mexico.
We _____ (we're)	
You _____ (you're)	
They _____ (they're)	

See Reference page 16

UNIT 1 **9**

Exchange information about your family

CAN DO ✓

GRAMMAR possessive *'s*; possessive adjectives; *yes/no* questions with *be*

Vocabulary | families

1 What are their relationships? Match the words and phrases to the photos.

_____ 1. father and sons   _____ 4. brothers
_____ 2. mother and daughter _____ 5. sisters
_____ 3. husband and wife

2 Match the sentence parts.

1. David Beckham is   a. Tom's wife.
2. Katie Holmes is   b. Serena's sister.
3. Venus Williams is   c. Brooklyn's father.
4. Cruz is   d. Madonna's daughter.
5. Lourdes is   e. Romeo's brother.

A Tom Katie

Grammar | possessive *'s*

3 Circle the correct sentence.

1. Tom is Katie husband.   2. Tom is Katie's husband.

See Reference page 16

4 **Pair Work** Make sentences about the photos. Use *'s*.

> *Madonna is Lourdes's mother.*

B Venus Serena

5 Match the family words to the meanings.

_*d*_ 1. mother and father   a. uncle
_____ 2. sons and daughters   b. grandmother
_____ 3. father's or mother's brother c. nephew
_____ 4. father's or mother's sister   d. parents
_____ 5. mother's or father's mother   e. aunt
_____ 6. mother's or father's father   f. niece
_____ 7. brother's or sister's son   g. children
_____ 8. brother's or sister's daughter h. grandfather

C Brooklyn Romeo David Cruz

Pronunciation | /ʌ/ sound

6a ▶1.10 Listen to the underlined sound /ʌ/. m<u>o</u>ther br<u>o</u>ther

b ▶1.11 Listen and repeat these family words. <u>Underline</u> the sound /ʌ/ in three words.

1. husband   4. father   7. nephew
2. uncle   5. cousin   8. sister-in-law
3. daughter   6. niece

D Lourdes Madonna

Grammar | possessive adjectives; yes/no questions with be

7 Read about the celebrities. Complete the Active Grammar box with the <u>underlined</u> words.

- Tom Cruise is an actor, and <u>his</u> wife is, too.
- Venus Williams is famous, and <u>her</u> sister is, too.
- David and Victoria Beckham love <u>their</u> children.

8 Fill in the blanks with possessive adjectives.

Ex: Claire is __our__ sister. (we)

1. _____ teacher is American. (I)
2. Mr. and Mrs. Simon are _____ parents. (they)
3. Which one is _____ sister? (he)
4. How old is _____ best friend? (you)
5. Are _____ sisters married? (she)

Active Grammar

Subject pronouns	Possessive adjectives
I	_my_
you	_your_
he	_____
she	_____
we	_our_
they	_____

See Reference page 16

9 Look at Exercise 8. Complete the Active Grammar box with *is* or *are*.

Active Grammar

	he she it	American?	Yes,	he she it	_____.	_____	we you they	American?	Yes,	we you they	_____.

See Reference page 16

Listening

10a Complete the sentences with *she, he, my, your, is,* or *are*. Then match the questions to the answers.

1. She's nice. Is she _____ mother?
2. She's young! How old _____ she?
3. And this man, is _____ your uncle?
4. Where _____ he from?
5. The girls are beautiful. Are they _____ sisters?
6. How old _____ they?

a. No. Claire's _____ sister and Liz _____ her best friend.
b. Well, she _____ 48.
c. No, he's _____ sister's boyfriend.
d. No, _____'s my mother-in-law, Jack's mother.
e. Claire _____ 18 and Liz _____ 22.
f. He _____ from Warsaw.

b ▶1.12 Listen and check your answers.

Speaking

11 **Pair Work** Write the names of five people in your family. Ask and answer questions.

Who's Elena?　　She's my aunt.　　Is she your mother's sister?

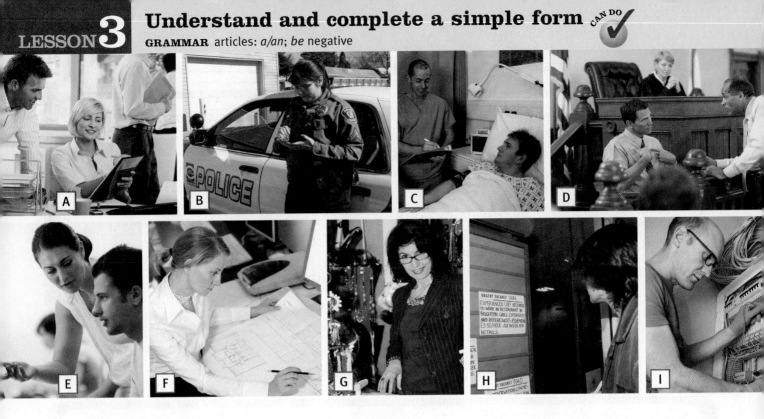

Vocabulary | jobs

1 **Pair Work** Match the photos with the words in the box. Discuss with a partner.

a banker	an artist	a dentist	a teacher	an assistant	a journalist
a nurse	a store clerk	retired	an architect	an electrician	a lawyer
a computer programmer		an engineer	unemployed	a student	a police officer

Grammar | *a/an*

2a Look at the jobs in the box in Exercise 1.
Complete the Active Grammar box with *a* or *an*.

b Write *a* or *an*. Ex: __*a*__ mother

1. _____ answer
2. _____ country
3. _____ uncle
4. _____ taxi
5. _____ family
6. _____ hand

> **Active Grammar**
>
> Use _____ before vowel sounds, such as *a, e,* and *i*. She's _____ artist.
>
> Use _____ before consonant sounds, such as *b, d,* and *f*. He's _____ lawyer.

See Reference page 16

Speaking

3 **Pair Work** Ask and answer questions about your partner's family or friends.

brother	mother	father
sister	uncle	best friend

Grammar | *be* negative

4 Complete the Active Grammar box with *'m not* and *isn't*.

> **Active Grammar**
>
> | I _____ | We aren't |
> |---|---|
> | He _____ | You aren't |
> | She _____ | They aren't |

See Reference page 16

5 Complete the sentences with the correct negative form of *be*.

   Ex: We ___*aren't*___ from the United States.

   1. My sister _____ married.
   2. I _____ a store clerk; I'm the manager.
   3. My cousins _____ at home.
   4. Uncle Jon is 70, but he _____ retired.

Reading

6 Look at this website form. Match the questions to the parts of the form.

   __3__ a. How old are you?

   _____ b. What's your (cell) phone number?

   _____ c. What's your last name?

   _____ d. What's your email address?

   _____ e. Where are you from?

   _____ f. What do you do?

   _____ g. What's your first name?

   _____ h. What's your address?

   _____ i. What's your nationality?

1. First name: Yuko
2. Last name:
3. Age:
4. Place of origin:
5. Nationality:
6. Address:

7. Email address:

8. Telephone number
   home:
   cell:
9. Occupation:

Listening

7a ▶1.13 Listen and complete the form in Exercise 6.

b **Pair Work** Check your answers with a partner.

> *What's her last name?*   *Noda. How old is she?*

Speaking

8 **SPEAKING EXCHANGE** Complete the forms below with a partner.

   Student A: Ask questions about the forms below.
   Student B: Look at page 127 and answer the questions.

1

First name: S E R E N A
Last name:
Age: 3 4
Place of origin: M E X I C O
Nationality:
Address: 1 2 H Y T H E S T R E E T
          L O N D O N
Email address:

Telephone number (home): 0 2 0 8 1 4 2 9 0 5 5
Telephone number (cell):
Occupation: L A W Y E R

2

First name:
Last name: L E E
Age:
Place of origin:
Nationality: C H I N E S E
Address:

Email address: C L E E 4 0 2 @ e i c l . c o m

Telephone number (home):
Telephone number (cell): 0 2 9 2 4 0 5 5 5 1
Occupation:

Review

1 Circle the correct <u>underlined</u> word.

> **Ex:** Excuse me. Is this *my/* (*your*) bag?

1. John is 12 and *his/her* sister is 14.
2. This is Mariana. She's *my/her* wife's best friend.
3. Mr. and Mrs. Silva are teachers, and *they/their* children are students.
4. We are Chinese. *Our/Their* parents are from Beijing.
5. Jennifer Lopez is American, but *her/their* parents are from Puerto Rico.
6. My sister is married. *His/Her* husband is 43.

2 **Pair Work** Take turns making sentences using the cues.

> **Ex:** Pilar and Esteban/Spain   *Pilar and Esteban are from Spain. They are Spanish.*

1. Elizabeth/Australia
2. Paula and Luis/Colombia
3. I/France
4. You/the United States
5. Steve/Canada
6. His camera/Japan

3 Complete the questions and answers. Use information from Exercise 2. Then practice with a partner.

> **Ex:** **A:** __Is_____ Elizabeth British?
> **B:** No, she _isn't_____. She's _Australian____.

A: _____ (1.) Paula and Luis from Mexico?

B: No, they _____ (2.). They _____ (3.) from _____ (4.).

A: _____ (5.) Steve _____ (6.) Canada?

B: Yes, he _____ (7.).

A: _____ (8.) his camera German?

B: _____ (9.), it _____. (10.) It's Japanese.

4 Complete the dialog with questions. Then practice with a partner.

> **Ex:** **A:** _Hi, what's your name?_____   **B:** My name's Andreas Schmidt.

A: _____ (1.)

B: Yes, it is, and Schmidt is my last name.

A: _____ (2.)

B: I'm from Germany.

A: _____ (3.)

B: I'm 23.

A: _____ (4.)

B: I'm an engineer . . . This is David and Gina.

A: _____ (5.)

B: They're my cousins.

A: _____ (6.)

B: No, they aren't. They're American. My aunt is married to an American.

Communication | start and finish a basic conversation

5a ▶1.14 Listen to two dialogs and check (✓) the expressions you hear.

_____ Excuse me . . .   _____ See you later.   _____ Hello.   _____ Hi.

_____ Good morning.   _____ See you tomorrow.   _____ Goodbye.   _____ Bye.

b Read the How To box.

> ### How To:
>
> ## Start and finish a basic conversation
>
> | Start | • _Hello._
• _Good morning._
• _Hi._
• _Excuse me . . ._ |
> |---|---|
> | Finish | • _See you tomorrow._
• _See you later._
• _Bye._
• _Goodbye._ |

6a Complete the dialogs with the phrases in the box.

> What do you do?   I'm from Rio.   Hello Maria, I'm Emi.
> Excuse me, are you Juan?   What's your email address?

1. **A:** Hi, I'm Maria.

   B: _____

   A: Nice to meet you.

2. **A:** _____

   B: Yes, I am. What's your name?

   A: My name's Jin.

3. **A:** Where are you from?

   B: _____

4. **A:** _____

   B: It's jin77@hotserve.com.

5. **A:** _____

   B: I'm a college student.

b ▶1.15 Listen and check your answers.

7 **Pair Work** Practice the dialogs in Exercise 6a with a partner. Use real information.

8a **Group Work** Talk with other students. Find:

- a college student.
- a student with an interesting job.
- a student with the letter "Y" in his or her name.
- a student with a funny email address.
- a student from an interesting place.

b Tell the class your results.

Ex: Pedro is a college student.

Unit 1 Reference

Subject pronouns, possessive adjectives, and possessive 's

There are eight subject pronouns in English. Use subject pronouns before verbs. There are also eight possessive adjectives. Use possessive adjectives before nouns.

Subject pronouns	I you he she it we you they	+ verb	Possessive adjectives	my your his her its our your their	+ noun

Possessive adjectives and noun + 's means *belongs to* (for things). With people they show relationships.

This is John's phone.   *This is **his** phone.*   *Peggy is Al's wife.*

Verb *be*

+	I	'm	German. / from Germany.			
	You	're				
	He / She / It	's				
	We / You / They	're				
−	I	'm not	Italian. / from Italy.			
	You	aren't				
	He / She / It	isn't				
	We / You / They	aren't				
?	Am	I	American?	Yes, (No.)	I	am. ('m not)
	Are	you			you	are. (aren't)
	Is	he / she / it			he / she / it	is. (isn't)
	Are	we / you / they			we / you / they	are. (aren't)

Informal English usually uses the contracted forms: 'm = am, 's = is, 're = are, isn't = is not, aren't = are not.

*I am Chinese. = **I'm** Chinese.   He is Brazilian. = **He's** Brazilian.*
*I'm not Italian. He/She/It **isn't** Italian. We/You/They **aren't** Italian.*

Do not use contracted forms in questions and short affirmative answers.

A: *Are you Korean?*   **B:** *Yes, I am.*

Wh- questions

Form *wh-* questions with a question word.

Who asks about a person.

What asks about a thing.

Where asks about a place.

When asks about a time.

How old asks about age.

Question word + *am/is/are* + subject pronoun.

Where *are you from?*

a/an

Use *a/an* to introduce singular nouns.
a teacher, an address

Use *a* before consonant sounds.
a burger, a handbag

Use *an* before vowel sounds.
an engineer, an uncle

Unit Vocabulary

Jobs

a nurse	a police officer
retired	a store clerk
a student	an assistant
an artist	an architect
a teacher	an electrician
a dentist	an engineer
a lawyer	a journalist
unemployed	
a computer programmer	

Family

Male:

	son	grandfather
brother	father	husband
nephew	uncle	stepfather
father-in-law		

Female:

	wife	daughter
mother	aunt	stepmother
sister	niece	grandmother
mother-in-law		

Male or female:

parents	children	cousins

UNIT 2
Work and leisure

Warm Up

1a Match an activity in the word box to a photo.

A go to work —— leave work —— have dinner —— have lunch —— get up

—— go to bed —— have breakfast —— go home —— leave home

b Match the activities from Exercise 1a to the times of the day.

 in the morning *get up,* _____

—— in the evening _____

—— in the afternoon _____

 at night _____

Reading

1 Match the advertisements to the descriptions.

ad for an all-inclusive vacation = _____

ad for a job = _____

Be a rep for

Club W Resorts

A fun job

for fun people!

• organize parties

• sell tickets for excursions

• help our guests

Call 1-800-555-0198 now!

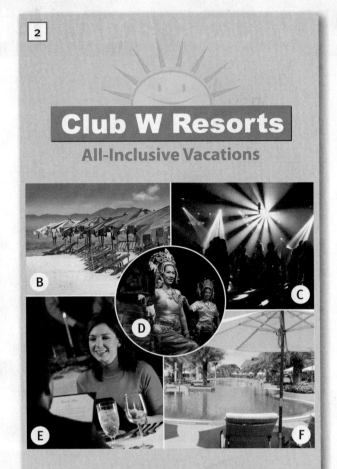

Club W Resorts

All-Inclusive Vacations

Hotel, food, and entertainment included in the price!

American English	British English
vacation	holiday

Vocabulary | vacations

2 Match the words to the pictures A–F.

_____ 1. restaurant   _____ 4. swimming pool

_____ 2. entertainment   _____ 5. beach

_____ 3. Club W rep   _____ 6. nightclub

Listening

3a ▶1.16 Listen and complete the times with the words in the box.

> a quarter past   thirty   a quarter to   o'clock

What time is it?

1. It's six _____.

3. It's three _____.

2. It's _____ five.

4. It's _____ eight.

b ▶1.17 Jenny is a Club W rep. Listen and check (✓) the eight activities she mentions.

_____ 1. get up

_____ 2. have breakfast

_____ 3. go to the hotel

_____ 4. tell guests about parties

_____ 5. have lunch

_____ 6. go to the office

_____ 7. organize games at the pool

_____ 8. take guests to a restaurant

_____ 9. go to a nightclub

_____ 10. get home

c Listen again. Write Jenny's activities and the times in the correct place in her datebook on the right.

d Write a datebook page about your daily routine.

Grammar | simple present: *I/you/we*

4 Look at the Audioscript on page 137 and complete the Active Grammar box.

Active Grammar	
⊕	Sometimes we _____ special parties.
Yes/no questions	Do you play the games?
	Yes, I _____.
	No, I _____.
Wh- questions	What do you do in the afternoon?
	Where _____ dinner?

See Reference page 26

Morning

1 *get up - 10:00*

2

3

Afternoon

4

5

Evening

6

7

8

5 Read the How To box.

6a Read the interview. Complete the dialog and write the job at the end.

A: When _____ (1.) you get up?

B: At ten in the evening.

A: _____ (2.) you work at night?

B: Yes, I do.

A: What _____ (3.) you _____ (4.) in the afternoon?

B: I sleep.

A: Where _____ (5.) you work?

B: I _____ (6.) in a hospital.

A: So, what do you do?

B: I'm a [_____] .

How To:	
Talk about your daily routine	
Ask about routines	*What do you do in the afternoon?*
Answer	*I sleep.*
Ask about times	*When do you get up?*
Answer	*At ten in the evening.*
Ask about places	*Where do you work?*
Answer	*I work in a hospital.*

b ▶1.18 **Pair Work** Listen and check your answers. Then practice the dialog with a partner.

Speaking

7 **Pair Work** Interview a partner about his or her daily routine.

[*What do you do in the morning?*]　[*Do you work in an office?*]　[*When do you have lunch?*]

Write about a daily routine

GRAMMAR simple present: *he/she/it*

① **Jo Kinsey** has an interesting job. She's a hairdresser—but a special one. Jo works at Madame Tussaud's—the <u>wax model</u> museum. In the morning she checks the models for dirty hair, and in the afternoon she washes and dries their hair.

② **Jeanette Jones** cleans the <u>shark</u> tank at the aquarium in her city. She swims underwater every day to clean the tank, and she feeds the sharks three times a week. The visitors at the aquarium watch her work.

③ **John Ward** invents rides for his theme park. He walks through the park and listens to people when they talk about <u>a ride</u>. He invents new rides, and engineers design them. John really likes his work!

Reading

1a **Pair Work** Look at the photos. What are the jobs?

b Read the articles quickly and check your answers.

1. _____ 2. _____ 3. _____

c Match the photos to the <u>underlined</u> words in the articles.

A. _____ B. _____ C. _____

Vocabulary | verbs

2 Write a verb from the articles under each picture.

| a | b | c | d |

_____ _____ _____ _____

| e | f | g |

_____ _____ _____

Grammar | simple present: *he/she/it*

3a Look at the verbs in the reading. Complete the Active Grammar box with *has, -s, or -es*.

b Complete the sentences with the correct form of the verbs in parentheses.

1. Jo _____ (wash) and
_____ (dry) the models' hair.
2. Jeanette _____ (clean) the shark tank.
3. John _____ (have) an interesting job.

See Reference page 26

> ### Active Grammar
>
> After *he, she,* and *it*, add _____ to the verb, but:
>
> 1. when the verb ends in *o, s, sh, ch,* or *x*, add _____.
> 2. when the verb ends in consonant + *y*, change *-y* to *-i* and add _____.
> 3. the form of *have* after *he, she,* and *it* is _____.

4 Complete the sentences with the correct form of the verbs in the box.

> clean   have   help   play   talk   wash   watch

1. My mother _____ our house.
2. The teacher _____ softly in class.
3. Jake _____ his hair every morning.
4. Matt _____ DVDs on his laptop computer.
5. Allie _____ her little sister with her homework.
6. My brothers _____ soccer on TV.
7. He _____ a dangerous job.

Pronunciation | verb endings

5a ▶1.19 Listen to the endings of these three verbs. Are they all the same?

/s/ walks	/z/ listens	/ɪz/ organizes

b ▶1.20 Listen and write the verbs in the correct column in the chart. Then repeat them.

Listening

6a Complete the dialog.

Ex: A: Does Jeanette like her work?   **B:** Yes, she does. She __*loves*__ it.

1. **A:** _____ she clean the tank every day?   **B:** Yes, she _____.
2. **A:** _____ she feed the sharks every day?   **B:** No. She _____ them three times a week.

b ▶1.21 **Pair Work** Listen and check your answers. Then practice the dialog with a partner.

Speaking

7 **SPEAKING EXCHANGE** Rob is a studio engineer. Ask and answer questions about his daily routine. Complete the datebook.

Student A: Look at the datebook on page 127.
Student B: Look at the datebook on page 131.

Vocabulary | everyday objects

1a Pair Work Look at the photo. Where are the people? Why are they there?

b ▶1.22 Listen and check your answers.

2a Label the objects in the picture.

bags	books	DVD player
lamps	pictures	shoes
suitcase	laptop computer	
watches	video camera	

b ▶1.23 Listen and check (✓) the objects you hear.

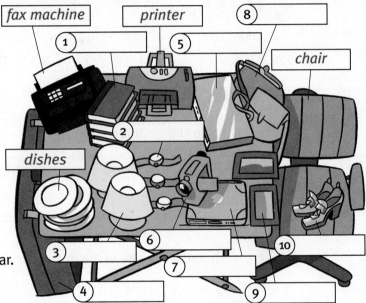

fax machine   *printer*   8

chair

1   5

2

dishes

6   10

3

7   9

4

Grammar | *this/that/these/those*

3 ▶1.24 Listen and complete the dialogs.

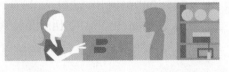

1. **A:** What's _____?
   B: It's _____.

3. **A:** What are _____?
   B: They're _____.

2. **A:** What's _____?
   B: It's _____.

4. **A:** What are _____?
   B: They're _____.

See Reference page 26

Pronunciation | short and long vowel sounds

4a ▶1.25 Listen to the vowel sounds. Repeat. /ɪ/ th<u>i</u>s   /i/ th<u>e</u>se

b ▶1.26 Listen and write these words in the correct column in the chart.

green   listen   niece   pink
read   sister   teacher   think

/ɪ/ this	/i/ these

Vocabulary | adjectives

5a **Pair Work** Match the opposite adjectives. Use a dictionary if needed.

~~bad~~   big   ~~good~~   awful   modern   nice   old
old-fashioned   small   useful   useless   young

bad – good

b **Pair Work** Take turns making sentences with the adjectives above.

> *My house is big, but my car is small.*

Listening

6a ▶1.27 Listen. Match the dialogs to the pictures below. 1. _____ 2. _____ 3. _____

b Look at the Audioscript on page 137. Label the objects in each suitcase.

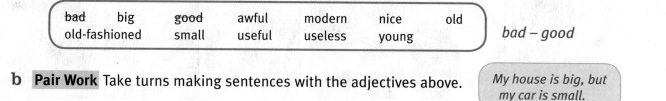

A _____ _____ B _____ _____ C _____

Grammar | plural nouns

7 Complete the Active Grammar box. Then complete the chart.

Active Grammar

one book, twenty _____

one lamp, ten _____

one phone, two _____

To make the regular plural of a noun, add _____.

See Reference page 26

regular	book, ___*books*___	shoe _____
noun + -es	watch, _____	dish _____
f → -ves	scarf, _____	wife _____
consonant -y → -ies	city, ___*cities*___	story _____
irregular	person, ___*people*___	woman _____

Speaking

8 **Pair Work** Play a guessing game. Ask *yes/no* questions. Guess the object. Use adjectives.

> *Do you use it every day?*   *Do you use it in class?*   *Is it a cell phone?*

Review

1 **Pair Work** Look at the pictures and take turns making sentences about Tom's day. Use the verbs and phrases in the box.

eat	read	the news	to bed	watch	a sandwich
go	~~take~~	work	his email	finish	~~the bus to work~~

A. *He takes the bus to work at a quarter past eight.*

B. _____

C. _____

D. _____

E. _____

F. _____

2 Complete the sentences with the correct form of the verbs in parentheses.

Ex: She __*finishes*__ work at five o'clock. (finish)

1. They _____ at ten o'clock on Sundays. (get up)

2. _____ he _____ a good job? (have)

3. I _____ to English lessons in the evening. (go)

4. She _____ the house in the morning. (clean)

3 Put the words in the correct order to make questions.

Ex: to / you / work / When / go / do / ? __*When do you go to work?*__

1. she / afternoon / What / does / do / in / the / ? _____

2. have / Where / does / lunch / he / ? _____

3. to / work / Do / take / the / train / you / ? _____

4. does / finish / he / When / work / ? _____

4 **Pair Work** Complete the questions and answers. Then practice with a partner.

What's __*this*__ ? What are _____ ? What's _____ ? _____ ? _____ ?

It's a They're It's a _____ _____

laptop computer . _____ . _____ . _____ . _____ .

Communication | ask questions
for information and understand the answers

5 Match the photos to the captions.

_____ 1. in the city

_____ 2. in the mountains

_____ 3. at the beach

6 Complete the questions in the questionnaire below with words from the box.

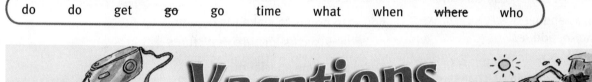

do   do   get   ~~go~~   go   time   what   when   ~~where~~   who

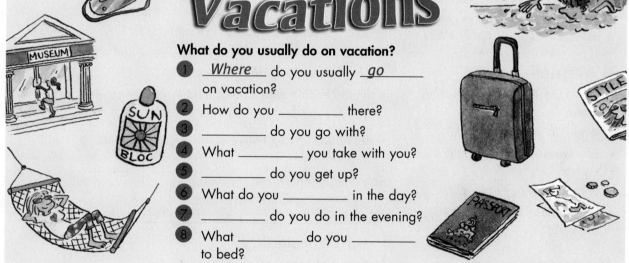

Vacations

What do you usually do on vacation?

1 _Where_ do you usually _go_ on vacation?

2 How do you _____ there?

3 _____ do you go with?

4 What _____ you take with you?

5 _____ do you get up?

6 What do you _____ in the day?

7 _____ do you do in the evening?

8 What _____ do you _____ to bed?

7 **Pair Work** Ask your partner about his or her usual vacation and write the answers.

> Where do you go usually go on vacation?

> I go to the beach.

8 **Group Work** Tell the group about your partner's usual vacation.

> Stefano usually goes to his sister's house in Miami.

Unit 2 Reference

Simple present

⊕	*I*	
	we	*take*
	you	
	they	
	he	
	she	*takes*
	it	

*I **take** the train.*
*She **takes** the bus.*

Use the simple present for daily routines and activities. With *I*, *we*, *you*, and *they*, the simple present form is the same as the base form of the verb. With *he*, *she*, and *it*, add -*s*, but note these exceptions:

- verbs ending in -*ch*, -*s*, -*sh*, -*x*, and -*o*, add -*es*
  watch → *watches, go* → *goes*

- verbs ending in -*y*, change -*y* to -*i* and add -*es*   *carry* → *carries*
  have is irregular   *have* → *has*

Wh- questions

- *Wh*- word + *do* + *I/we/you/they* + verb (base form)
  When do you finish work?

- *Wh*- word + *does* + *he/she/it* + verb
  Where does he eat lunch?

- In questions, don't add -*s* to the verb.

Yes/no questions

- *Do* + *I/we/you/they* + verb
  Do you eat with clients?

- *Does* + *he/she/it* + verb
  Does he finish at five o'clock?

- Note the short answers:
  Yes, I/we/you/they do.
  he/she/it does.

  No, I/we/you/they don't.
  he/she/it doesn't.

this, that, these, those

	Singular	Plural
Near	*this*	*these*
Far	*that*	*those*

*What's **this**?*   *Do you like **these** shoes?*   *Look at **that** car!*   ***Those** bags are nice.*

Plural nouns

Add -*s* to nouns to make the regular noun plural.
  book → *books, picture* → *pictures*

There are some special rules:

- nouns ending in -*ch*, -*s*, -*sh*, and -*x*, add -*es*
  watch → *watches, address* → *addresses*

- most nouns ending in -*f*, change -*f* to -*v* and add -*es*
  scarf → *scarves, knife* → *knives*

- nouns ending with a consonant + -*y*, change -*y* to -*i* and add -*es*
  diary → *diaries, city* → *cities*

Note: nouns ending with a vowel + -*y* are regular.
  day → *days*

Some plural nouns are irregular.
  man → *men, child* → *children*

Unit Vocabulary

Personal possessions

car	lamp	watch	camera	suitcase	DVD player
bag	book	purse	wallet	datebook	fax machine
dish	chair	shoes	picture	magazine	video camera
desk	scarf	printer	scissors	cell phone	laptop computer

Basic verbs/verb phrases

Routines: clean · eat · wash · have breakfast/lunch/dinner
get up · sleep · finish · start · go to home/work/school/bed
watch · work · leave home/work

Other verbs: check · repair · feed · dry · like
design · invent · open · walk · help · sell
organize · listen · swim · meet · play

UNIT 3
Your free time

Warm Up

1a Circle the phrases in the box that match the photos.

go to a concert	go for a walk	go shopping	read a book or magazine
go to the gym	listen to music	meet friends	watch TV or a DVD
play the guitar	sunbathe	swim	cook dance

b Where do you do the activities in Exercise 1a? Write them in the chart.

At home	At a park	At a mall	At a nightclub	At a concert hall	At a sports center

TRAFFIC JAMS. WE HATE THEM, BUT WHAT DO WE DO IN THEM?

Listening

1 ▶1.28 Listen and complete the quotes below about traffic jams. Compare your answers with a partner. Then listen again and check.

"Traffic jams are OK. I think about work and _____ (1.) my day. <u>My daughter doesn't like traffic jams</u> — she calls her friends, but I don't make phone calls in the car." (*Carla, 39*)

"I don't do a lot, really. I _____ (3.) traffic jams—they're so boring! I think about things or _____ (4.) the people in the other cars. Sometimes I sing." (*Hiro, 35*)

"I shave and listen to the radio. I _____ (2.) the news. Unfortunately my car doesn't have a CD player." (*Gary, 28*)

"We _____ (5.) or _____ (6.) friends on our cell phones. Or we just talk. We don't usually listen to music." (*Lauren, 22, and Emily, 21*)

Grammar | simple present: negative

2a Read the following sentences. Find and <u>underline</u> the negative forms of these sentences in Exercise 1.

> **Ex:** My daughter likes traffic jams.

1. I make phone calls in the car.
2. My car has a CD player.
3. We usually listen to music.

b Complete the Active Grammar box with *don't* or *doesn't*.

c **Pair Work** What about you? Read the sentences aloud. Correct the false sentences.

> **Ex:** I like traffic jams. *I don't like traffic jams.*

1. I listen to the news on the radio.
2. I go shopping on weekends.
3. I make phone calls in the car.
4. I sleep for ten hours every night.

Active Grammar

I	_____
He/She/It	_____ work.
We/You/They	_____

See Reference page 36

Listening

3 ▶1.29 Listen to Carlos talking about his activities. Write the days.

Tuesday

Reading

4a Read the article about Carlos. Find three mistakes with the days and correct them.

b **Pair Work** Take turns making positive or negative sentences about Carlos. Use the corrected article to help you.

    Ex: Mondays/play tennis

> He doesn't play tennis on Mondays.

1. Thursdays/watch a movie
2. Fridays/work
3. Saturdays/play soccer
4. Sundays/sleep

Speaking

5a Read the questionnaire. Check (✓) the things you do, and write the day you do them, if possible. Then add two more.

b **Pair Work** Complete the questionnaire for your partner.

Writing

6 Write a short article about your free time. Use your notes from Exercise 5a. Start your article with a short introduction.

> My name is . . . I work in . . . , but I do a lot of things in my free time. On Mondays, I . . .

What I do on my lunch break

Today we talk to Carlos Lopez. Carlos works in the city. He doesn't go home at lunchtime, so how does he spend his time?

"Well, I have an hour and I want to use that time," says Carlos. He certainly does! On Mondays, Carlos goes for a walk or goes swimming. On Tuesdays, he sometimes meets friends, and they have lunch at a restaurant. On Wednesdays, he goes to the gym. On Thursdays, he sometimes listens to a lunchtime concert. On Fridays, he goes shopping.

Activity	You (when)	Your partner (when)
talk to friends on the phone		
watch TV		
listen to music		
play computer games		
go for walks		
play a sport		
go to concerts	✓ (Friday evenings)	
go to the movies		
read books		
go to the gym		

Talk about what you can and can't do

GRAMMAR *can/can't*: ability

Vocabulary | sports and games

1a Match the words in the box to the pictures below.

> aerobics soccer running karate computer games
> sailing yoga skiing tennis swimming

b Write the activities in the chart. Then check the Unit Vocabulary on page 36.

Do	Go	Play
do aerobics	*go running*	*play soccer*

American English	British English
soccer	football

c **Pair Work** Ask and answer questions about the activities.

Reading

2a **Pair Work** Read the introduction to the article. Then ask and answer the questions with a partner.

1. Where is Tony Hawk from?
2. What does he do?
3. Some people think he is unusual. Why?

b **Pair Work** Read the article on page 31. Then ask and answer the questions.

> **Ex:** How old is Tony? *He is 43.*

1. How many prizes does he have?
2. What does he do on his skateboard?
3. What does he write?
4. What kind of show does he have?
5. Can he play the guitar?

Tony Hawk
the man and the board

Tony Hawk is American. He's 43. He has four children. He's a businessman. And he's one of the top skateboarders in the world.

Grammar | *can/can't*

3 Complete the sentences and questions with *can* or *can't*. Then complete the Active Grammar box.

> **Ex:** What __can__ Tony Hawk do?
>
> 1. He _____ skateboard.
> 2. What _____ his friends do?
> 3. They _____ play the guitar and sing.
> 4. _____ you skateboard?
> 5. No, I _____, but I _____ ride a bike.

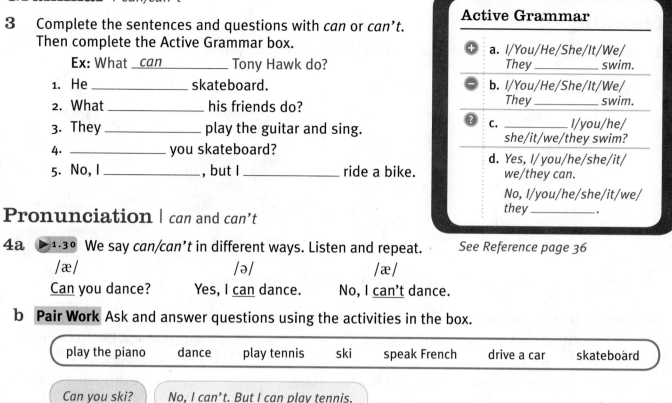

Active Grammar

➕ **a.** I/You/He/She/It/We/They _____ swim.

➖ **b.** I/You/He/She/It/We/They _____ swim.

❓ **c.** _____ I/you/he/she/it/we/they swim?

d. Yes, I/you/he/she/it/we/they can.

No, I/you/he/she/it/we/they _____ .

See Reference page 36

Pronunciation | *can* and *can't*

4a ▶ **1·30** We say *can/can't* in different ways. Listen and repeat.

/æ/   /ə/   /æ/

<u>Can</u> you dance?   Yes, I <u>can</u> dance.   No, I <u>can't</u> dance.

b **Pair Work** Ask and answer questions using the activities in the box.

> play the piano   dance   play tennis   ski   speak French   drive a car   skateboard

> *Can you ski?*   *No, I can't. But I can play tennis.*

Speaking

5 **Group Work** Look at the *can* and *can't* lists below. Stand and ask your classmates questions to find someone who:

Tony has 73 prizes from skateboarding competitions. He's 43 but he can skateboard like a 16-year-old. He can go very fast, and he does tricks on his skateboard.

But Tony isn't only a fantastic skateboarder—he can do other things, too. Tony writes books and computer games. *HAWK—Occupation: skateboarder* is a bestseller in the United States.

Tony also has a skateboarding and music show. He doesn't perform the music—he can't play the guitar or sing—but he and other skateboarders perform tricks, and musicians play rock music. The show is very popular.

can . . .
- speak three languages
- stand on their head
- write backwards
- move their ears
- play an unusual instrument
- do karate

can't . . .
- cook
- swim
- sing
- write with their right hand
- get up in the mornings
- send a text message

Understand and leave a simple phone message

FUNCTIONS requests and suggestions: *Let's/How about . . . ?/Why don't we . . . ?*; using the phone

Listening

1 Pair Work Do you use a cell phone? Where? When? Who do you call?

2a ▶1.31 Listen and complete the messages with a word, a number, or a time.

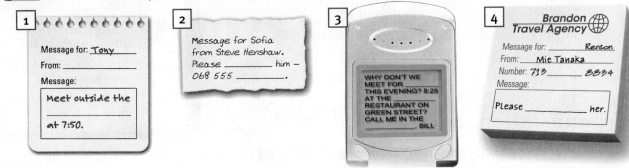

1.
Message for: _Tony_____
From: _____
Message:
Meet outside the
_____
at 7:50.

2.
Message for Sofia
from Steve Henshaw.
Please _____ him –
068 555 _____.

3.
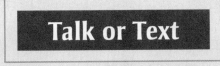
WHY DON'T WE
MEET FOR
THIS EVENING? 8:25
AT THE
RESTAURANT ON
GREEN STREET?
CALL ME IN THE
_____. BILL

4.
Brandon Travel Agency
Message for: _____ Renton
From: __Mie Tanaka___
Number: 713_____ 8834
Message:
Please _____ her.

b Listen to message 4 again. How is *88* said in the phone number? _____

3a ▶1.32 Number the sentences in the correct order. Then listen and check.

_____ OK. What's your number?

_____ OK. Bye.

_____ She isn't here right now. Can I take a message?

_1___ Hello.

_____ Yes, please ask her to call Jeffrey.

_____ It's 555-908-5561.

_____ Hi, can I speak to Laura, please?

b Pair Work Practice the dialog with a partner.

4a SPEAKING EXCHANGE Make two phone calls with a partner. Then change roles.

Student A: Turn to page 127.   **Student B:** Read the notes below.

CALL 1 Your name is Carla. Call Student A: You want to speak to Jason. Your number is 990-555-0188.

CALL 2 Answer the phone and start the conversation. (Sylvia isn't here today. Take a message.)

b Pair Work Practice calling and leaving messages for friends and family.

Reading

5 Read the article. Write the number for each item.

_____ 1. cell phone users in the United States

_____ 2. text messages the average American sends or gets a month

_____ 3. text messages sent in the US each month

_____ 4. text messages the average teen sends or gets a month

Talk or Text

There are 290 million cell phone users in the United States. What do they use their cell phones for most? Texting. On average, each cell phone user in the United States sends and receives about 350 text messages each month. This adds up to a total of about 75 billion text messages sent in one month. Who texts the most? American teens. The average teen sends and receives almost 2,000 text messages a month. In fact, a recent study finds that American teens text their friends more often than they email, phone, or talk face-to-face with them.

6 ▶ 1·33 How do we say these numbers? Choose from the words in the box. Then listen and check your answers.

> sixty   six million   six thousand   sixty thousand   six billion
> ~~six~~   sixteen   six hundred   six hundred thousand

6 _six_ _____   16 _____   60 _____   600 _____

6,000 _____   60,000 _____   600,000 _____

6,000,000 _____   6,000,000,000 _____

Pronunciation | stress in numbers

7a ▶ 1·34 Listen. <u>Underline</u> the stressed sounds.   sixteen   sixty   fourteen   forty

b ▶ 1·35 Listen and check (✓) the number you hear.

1. fourteen ☐ / forty ☐
2. eighteen ☐ / eighty ☐
3. seventeen ☐ / seventy ☐
4. thirteen ☐ / thirty ☐
5. nineteen ☐ / ninety ☐
6. sixteen ☐ / sixty ☐

c **Pair Work** Test your partner. Say a number. Your partner writes the number.

8 Read the How To box.

How To:	
Make suggestions and requests	
Make suggestions	*Let's* + verb (base form) *Let's meet outside the theater at ten to eight.*
	Why don't we + verb (base form) + ? *Why don't we meet for dinner?*
	How about + noun + ? *How about the Italian restaurant on Green Street?*
Make requests	*Can you* + verb (base form) + ? *Can you ask him to call?*

See Reference page 36

9 Complete these suggestions and requests. Write the times in words.

> **Ex:** we meet / theater / 7:00?   Why _don't we meet at the theater at seven_ ?

1. have dinner / Chinese restaurant / 8:40
   Let's _____
   _____ .

2. you come / the office tomorrow / 9:55?
   Can _____
   _____ ?

3. 3:10 / Greek café / Belmont Street?
   How _____
   _____ ?

4. we go / the nightclub / 10:45?
   Why _____
   _____ ?

10a What do you like to do in the evening? Check (✓) the activities.

____ see a movie   ____ go to a concert   ____ go to a soccer game   ____ go to the gym
____ get take-out   ____ go to a nightclub   ____ have dinner at a restaurant

b **Pair Work** Work in pairs. You want to do something together tonight. Make suggestions. Then change partners and practice again. Use the How To box.

Review

1 **Pair Work** Take turns making positive or negative sentences about the photo below.

Ex: sleep in the park   *He sleeps in the park.*

1. have a job
2. have an address
3. go to work every morning
4. carry his things in a bag
5. eat in restaurants
6. like his life

2 Write a sentence with *can* and *can't* about the things below. Use words and phrases in the box. Then share your sentences with a partner.

drive	send photos
think	sleep all day
run	swim
send text messages	
check your spelling	
play computer games	

Ex: Children _can play computer games, but they can't drive._
1. Computers _____
2. Sharks _____
3. Cell phones _____
4. Cats _____

3 Put the words in order to make suggestions and requests.

Ex: movies / to / we / tonight / Why / don't / go / the / ?   _Why don't we go to the movies tonight?_

1. six o'clock / Let's / at / meet / . _____
2. restaurant / How / the / lunch / at / about / Italian / ? _____
3. a / Can / message / you / take / ? _____
4. give / your / Can / number / you / me / phone / ? _____
5. we / video / don't / watch / a / Why / ? _____
6. Saturday / about / on / How / dinner / ? _____

4 Complete the datebook with the correct verbs.

Monday
   play _____ soccer with the boys
1. _____ to the movies (evening)

Tuesday
2. _____ Jack and Ellie for lunch
3. _____ our bikes to the park

Wednesday
4. _____ to the gym
5. _____ dinner for Emma

Thursday
6. _____ to a nightclub
7. _____ the piano for Sam

Friday
8. _____ yoga with Jane (morning)
9. _____ swimming with the girls

Saturday
10. _____ shopping

Sunday
11. _____ Harry's video

Communication | talk about other people's abilities

5 Match the abilities to the jobs. Use a dictionary if necessary.

ABILITIES	JOBS
1. speak foreign languages	a. tennis coach
2. design buildings	b. taxi driver
3. play tennis	c. artist
4. drive	d. carpenter
5. repair computers	e. mechanic
6. play a musical instrument	f. photographer
7. draw and paint	g. tour guide
8. repair cars	h. musician
9. use a camera	i. architect
10. make things with wood	j. computer technician

6a Read the information below about Jane. Complete the employment agency notes on the right.

Jane Danby is 32 years old. She has a degree in art from Columbia University. She can speak Spanish and Chinese. She can paint and draw. She likes the Internet. She takes digital photos and she changes them on her computer. She can't drive.

PERFECT EMPLOYMENT AGENCY

Applicant notes

NAME: ....Jane Danby.......

AGE: ....

DEGREES:

....

ABILITIES:

....

....

LIKES/DISLIKES:

....

PERFECT EMPLOYMENT AGENCY

Applicant notes

NAME: ...David Burford.......

AGE: ....

DEGREES:

....

ABILITIES:

....

....

LIKES/DISLIKES:

....

b ▶1.36 Listen and complete the notes for David.

7a **Group Work** Work in groups of three. One of you works for the Perfect Employment Agency. The other two, Jane and David, want new jobs. Choose the best job for each person. Talk about your reasons and complete the chart.

> *I think "computer technician" is best for David.*   *Really? Why?*   *Because he has a degree in . . .*

Name		
Job		
Reasons		

b **Group Work** Compare your ideas with another group.

Unit 3 Reference

Simple present: negative

Form the negative of the simple present with the verb *do* + *not* + the base form of the verb.

I		
You	*don't*	
We	*(do not)*	
They		*work.*
He		
She	*doesn't*	
It	*(does not)*	

*I **don't live** in the city.*
*She **doesn't work** in the office.*

Note: Do not add *-s* to the verb in the simple present negative.

can/can't

Can is a modal. Use modals before other verbs. Modals do not change their form after *he*, *she*, or *it*.

The negative of *can* is *cannot*, but the short form *can't* is usually used.

I		
You		
He		
She	*can*	
It	*can't*	*sing.*
We	*(cannot)*	
You		
They		

*He **can play** the piano.*

Use *can* and *can't* to talk about ability. Use *can* to talk about things that one is able to do, and *can't* to talk about things that one is not able to do.

*I **can sing** but **I can't dance**.*

Making requests and suggestions

Use *can* + *you* + verb to make requests—when we want someone else to do something.

Can you take *a message?*

To do something with another person, make suggestions.

Let's + verb
Let's meet *outside the theater at ten to eight.*

Why don't we + verb + ?
Why don't we have *dinner this evening?*

How about + noun + ?
How about lunch *on Friday?*

play, do, go + activities

Use *play* + noun for games and for sports that are usually done in teams.

play soccer, computer games

Use *do* + noun for activities that can be done alone (not in a team).

do aerobics, yoga

Use *go* with activity verbs that end in *-ing*.

go swimming, running

Unit Vocabulary

Activities
cook
dance
do aerobics/karate/yoga
drive a car
get take-out
go for a walk
go running/sailing/shopping/skiing/swimming
go to the movies/a concert/the gym/a nightclub/
   a soccer game
have lunch/dinner (at a restaurant)
listen to music/the news/the radio
meet friends
play computer games/soccer/tennis
play the guitar/piano
read a book/a magazine
ride a bike
see a movie
sing
skateboard
sunbathe
swim
watch TV/DVD

UNIT 4
Food

A

B

C

D

Warm Up

1   **Pair Work** Which foods in the word box can you see in each photo?

| beef | bread | butter | cheese | chicken | fish | grapes | onions |
| lettuce | melon | milk | rice | strawberries | tea | tomatoes | tuna |

2   Complete the chart below with foods from Exercise 1 and other foods you know.

Meat/Fish	Dairy	Fruit	Drinks	Vegetables	Starches
		melon			

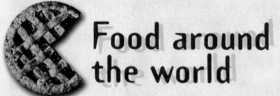

Food around the world

Megan and Craig Wilson and their children Andrea, 5, and Ryan, 3, live in California. Megan and Craig both work and they don't usually have time to cook, so they like easy-to-prepare food. The children love hot dogs, pizza, and cereal. The family often eats at fast food restaurants.

The Ukitas live in Tokyo, Japan. Kazuo Ukita lives with his wife, Sumi, and his daughters Mika, 17, and Maya, 14. Kazuo works for a car company. Sumi cooks breakfast before Kazuo leaves for work at 7:00 A.M. They have dinner together at home in the evenings. They eat a lot of fish and rice. Sumi cooks all the meals for her family.

Ramón Garcia, his wife Sandra, and their children Alexandra, 16, and Fabio, 6, live in Quito. Ecuador is a tropical country, so they eat a lot of fresh fruit—mangoes, pineapples, bananas, and papayas. They also eat a lot of fresh vegetables, potatoes, rice, and meat.

Vocabulary | food and drink

1   Look at the photo and find these things.

____ carrots	*A* ground beef	____soda
____ cereal	____ bottled water	
____ bananas	____ orange juice	

Reading

2   Read the article and check (✓) the correct answers.

Which family:	Wilson	Ukita	Garcia
1. eats a lot of fish?	☐	☐	☐
2. eats a lot of fresh fruit?	☐	☐	☐
3. eats a lot of rice?	☐	☐	☐
4. eats fast food?	☐	☐	☐
5. has dinner together?	☐	☐	☐

Grammar | count and noncount nouns; *How much?/How many?*

3a Look at the picture and answer the questions.

1. Can you count the eggs? _____

2. Can you count the cereal? _____

3. Which is the noncount noun, *eggs* or *cereal*? _____

b Here is the Wilson family's shopping list.

1. (Circle) the correct choices.
   a. The red words are _count/noncount_ nouns.
   b. The blue words are _count/noncount_ nouns.
   c. Noncount nouns do not have _singular/plural_ forms.
2. How do we measure noncount nouns? _____

Shopping list:
- 12 hot dogs
- a box of cereal
- 12 eggs
- a carton of milk
- 1 pound of ground beef

c Write the following headings in the Active Grammar box: Noncount nouns, Count nouns

Active Grammar

1. _____
- They have singular and plural forms.
- We can use numbers in front of them.

2. _____
- They do not have plural forms.
- We cannot use numbers in front of them.
- We often use quantity words (*a box, a pound*) + *of* in front of them.

See Reference page 46

4a Here are the shopping lists for the Garcia and Ukita families. Write the food in the chart.

Garcia
- 1 ~~pineapple~~
- 1 ~~loaf of bread~~
- 2 packages of rice
- 3 papayas
- 500g/1 lb coffee
- 12 bananas
- 1 box of cereal

Ukita
- 1 bag of rice
- 1 carton of milk
- 2 pizzas
- 1 can of tuna
- 12 eggs
- 500g/1 lb ground beef
- 3 tomatoes
- 2 bottles of soda

Count	Noncount
pineapple	bread

b Answer the questions. Then complete the Active Grammar box with *much* or *many*.

1. How much coffee does the Garcia family buy each week? _____
2. How many pineapples do they buy? _____

Active Grammar

a. Use *How* _____ with count nouns.
b. Use *How* _____ with noncount nouns.

See Reference page 46

5a Complete the dialog with words and phrases from the box.

coffee	much
tomatoes	six
two boxes	

A: How _____ (1.) cereal do you buy each week?
B: I usually buy _____ (2.) of cereal.
A: And how many _____ (3.) do you buy?
B: About _____ (4.).
A: How much _____ (5.) do you buy?
B: I buy one pound of coffee.

b ▶1·37 **Pair Work** Listen and check your answers. Then practice with a partner.

LESSON **2**
Talk about your diet and lifestyle CAN DO ✓
GRAMMAR indefinite quantities: *a/an/some/any*

Vocabulary | containers

1a Pair Work Look at the ad and discuss the questions.

1. What is the TV show about?
2. Who hosts the show?
3. Which food in the picture is healthy? Which food is unhealthy?

b Find and circle examples of these containers in the picture. Use a dictionary to help you.

bag	bottle	carton
box	can	package

In the garbage can

People's garbage tells us about their lives. Tonight Lisa Redburn looks at the diet of two families.

Tuesday 9:00 P.M. Channel 6

American English	British English
garbage can	rubbish bin

Listening

2a ▶1.38 Listen to the first part of the TV show. Write *a* or *b* by the correct garbage can.

b Listen again. Write the names of foods and drinks in the correct column.

Healthy food	Unhealthy food
vegetables	burgers
pasta	chips

Speaking

3 Pair Work Discuss.

1. Do you agree with Lisa about the diets of the two families?
2. What other food do you think is healthy/unhealthy?

Grammar | *a/an/some/any*

4 Look at these sentences. Complete the Active Grammar box with *a/an, some,* or *any*.

We have some cans . . .
We have a bottle . . .
Do they eat any vegetables or any fruit?
They eat some pasta . . .

Active Grammar

Noun	Singular count	Plural count	Noncount
⊕	_____	_____	_____
⊖	a/an	any	any
?	a/an	_____	any

See Reference page 46

5 Complete the sentences with *a/an, some,* or *any*.

Ex: We don't have __any__ potatoes.

1. I want _____ potatoes and _____ carrots, please.
2. Can I have _____ apple now?
3. I have _____ fruit here—do you want _____ banana?
4. We don't eat _____ meat.

Pronunciation | /æ/ and /ʌ/

6a ▶ 1.39 Listen to the vowel sounds in these words. Can you hear the difference?

/æ/	/ʌ/
have	some

b ▶ 1.40 Listen. <u>Underline</u> the /æ/ and /ʌ/ sounds in these sentences. Then repeat them.

1. He has lunch on Sundays at his club.
2. My family travels by taxi, but my young cousin takes the bus.
3. Anne and Sally have honey on their fruit salad.

Reading

7a Lisa writes about diet in a magazine. Read the letters to Lisa and match them to the problems.

_____ 1. He/She doesn't have time to cook.

_____ 2. He/She eats a lot.

_____ 3. He/She feels tired all the time.

A

Dear Lisa,
I'm always hungry. I eat three good meals a day, but then I want chips and cookies, too. Of course, now I'm quite fat! Can you help me?

Lois

B

Dear Lisa,
I know I have an unhealthy diet. I work about ten hours a day and I get home late, so I don't have time to cook and I eat fast food. What can I do?

James

C

Dear Lisa,
I try to eat a good diet—I eat pasta and vegetables, and I don't eat any meat, fish, or cheese—but I'm always tired. What's wrong with my diet?

Karin

b Read Lisa's answer to one letter.

1. Which letter does it answer? _____
2. How does she introduce her answer? _____
3. How does she make the two suggestions? _____
   _____

Dear _____,
It's awful when you feel tired all the time. You need some meat, fish, or cheese in your diet—they give you energy. Also, why don't you get more exercise? That gives you energy, too. How about a walk every evening after work? I hope that helps.

Lisa

Writing

8a Read the letters again and look at Lisa's notes below. Which notes are for which letter?

___B___ 1. salads are quick and healthy

_____ 2. eat fruit, not chips and cookies

_____ 3. go to the doctor

_____ 4. don't work ten hours a day

_____ 5. some foods cook quickly, such as fresh pasta

_____ 6. eat small meals

b **Group Work** Make more suggestions for the writers of the two letters.

c **Pair Work** In pairs, write an answer to letter A or B.

1. Think of two or three suggestions.
2. Write an introduction, your suggestions, and a closing.
3. Give your letter to another pair to correct and make suggestions.

Listening

1 **Group Work** Discuss.
  1. What kind of place does the photo show?
  2. Do you eat at places like these? Which ones?

2a ▶1.41 Listen to a dialog in a café. Who orders these things? Write *T* for Tracey and *S* for Sam.

_____ ham and cheese sandwich   _____ fries
_____ salad   _____ coffee   _____ bottled water

b Listen again and complete the bill on the right.

```
              🍴
          Restaurant
=================================

Ham and cheese sandwich  x1 $4.50

Large _____ (1)      x1 $3.00

_____ (2) salad      x1 $4.00

_____ (3) coffee     x1 $2.95

Small bottled _____ (4) x1 $2.25


TOTAL                    $_____(5)

Service & tax included
```

3a Below is the menu from a café. Match the headings to A–C.

_____ Drinks   _____ Main dishes   _____ Side orders

A _____	B _____	C _____
Sandwiches	**Regular fries** $____	**Regular coffee** $____
Ham and cheese $____	**Large fries** $____	**Large coffee** $____
Chicken salad $____	**Small salad** $____	**Orange juice** $____
Tuna salad $____	**Medium salad** $____	**Regular soda** $____
(white or whole wheat bread)	**Large salad** $____	**Large soda** $____
Burgers and pizzas		**Small bottled water** $____
Burger $____		**Large bottled water** $____
Vegetarian pizza $____		
Pepperoni pizza $____		

b **SPEAKING EXCHANGE**
  Student A: Turn to page 127.   **Student B:** Ask your partner questions to complete the menu.

  How much is a burger?   *A burger is three ninety-five.*

Grammar | object pronouns

4a ▶1.42 Listen and complete the sentences.

1. OK. A large cup of coffee for _____ and a small bottled water for _____ .

2. No, that's not for _____ .

3. Vegetarian pizzas? I really like _____ !

4. A medium salad for _____ ?

5. Oh, no, the salad's for _____ .

b Use the answers from Exercise 4a to complete the Active Grammar box.

Active Grammar

Subject pronouns	Object pronouns
I	_me_
he	_____
she	_____
it	_it_
we	_____
you	_____
they	_____

See Reference page 46

5 Tell the server. Complete the sentences with the correct object pronouns.

Well, who is this for?

Ex: you: "It isn't for _me_____ ."

1. your boyfriend: "It isn't for _____ ."

2. your mother: "It isn't for _____ ."

3. you and your friend: "It isn't for _____ ."

4. your brother and sister: "It isn't for _____ ."

6a Read the How To box.

b **Pair Work** Use the words in the box to complete the dialog. Then practice with a partner.

I'd	much	do	like	want	can

How To:

Order in a cafe restaurant

Ask questions	Do you have salads?
Say what you want	I'd like a cheese sandwich, please.
Ask about prices	How much is that?

A: What _____ (1.) I get for you today?

B: _____ (2.) like a vegetarian burger, please.

A: Any side orders?

B: _____ (3.) you have salads?

A: No, we don't. Do you _____ (4.) fries?

B: OK. Small fries.

A: Anything to drink?

B: Yes, I'd _____ (5.) an orange juice, please.

A: OK.

B: How _____ (6.) is that?

A: That's $10.95.

Speaking

7 **Group Work** Work in groups of three. Use the menu in Exercise 3a on page 42.

Student A: You are a server. Take the customers' order.

Students B and C: You are customers. Look at the menu and order a meal.

What can I get you today?   I'd like a salad.

Review

1   Match the sentence parts to make complete sentences.

1. I usually get a
2. We often get two
3. She puts some
4. I drink a carton
5. We need a can of
6. He gives me a box

a. tuna for this recipe.
b. of chocolates on Valentine's Day.
c. of milk every day.
d. pizza on Friday evening.
e. bags of chips at the supermarket.
f. cheese in the omelette.

2   Circle the correct choice.

Ex: How *much*/*many* oranges do you eat?

1. How *much*/*many* students are in the class?
2. She drinks three bottles of *waters*/*water* every day.
3. Let's have *four*/*a bag* of those nice brown eggs.
4. How *much*/*many* money do you have?
5. How *many*/*much* sugar do you eat every week?

3   Sherri phones her husband, but he doesn't answer. Complete her message with *a, some,* or *any.*

"Hello John. Oh, no, it's a message. He isn't there. Mmm. John, please listen to this message. Can you go to the store and get ___some___ things for dinner? We need _____ (1.) fish and _____ (2.) carton of eggs. Mmm, I think we have _____ (3.) potatoes, but we don't have _____ (4.) onions. Do we have _____ (5.) carrots? Can you check? Please buy _____ (6.) cheese, and I'd like _____ (7.) carton of orange juice. That's it. Oh . . . we don't have _____ (8.) butter — can you get some? Thanks. See you later."

4   **Pair Work** Replace the words in parentheses with the correct pronouns.

Ex: (Mr. Jones) takes (my friend and me) to work in his car.

> *He takes us to work in his car.*

1. (My mother and I) go shopping with (Julia and Carol) every Saturday.
2. (David and Serena) don't drive (the children) to school.
3. (My uncle) uses (the computer) every day.
4. (My friend and I) have lunch with (Maria) every Tuesday.

5   Put the letters in the correct order to write the names of food.

Ex: nolem   m_*elon*_____

1. ntau   t_____
2. errbug   b_____
3. eabrd   b_____
4. tware   w_____

5. otmotsea   t_____
6. ckechin   c_____
7. ilmk   m_____
8. crie   r_____

Communication | shop for food at a market

6a ▶1·43 Listen. What does the woman ask for? Check (✓) the blue boxes.

- ☐ ☐ apples
- ☐ ☐ bananas
- ☐ ☐ beef
- ☐ ☐ carrots
- ☐ ☐ chicken
- ☐ ☐ melon
- ☐ ☐ pork
- ☐ ☐ potatoes
- ☐ ☐ tomatoes
- ☐ ☐ tuna

b Listen again. What things can she buy? Check (✓) the pink boxes.

7a ▶1·44 Listen to the intonation. Write ↗ if it goes up and ↘ if it goes down.

I'd like three bananas ↗, six apples _____, and a melon _____, please. I'd like two pounds of ground beef _____, a pound of ground pork _____, and a whole chicken _____, please.

b Listen again and repeat.

c **Group Work** Play a game in groups. Choose food and drinks from the box below. Follow the example, and be careful to use the correct intonation.

apples	fish	carrots	pork	butter	ice cream	papayas	potatoes
pasta	eggs	coffee	tea	melons	bananas	tomatoes	pineapples
water	lamb	cheese	milk	chicken	ground beef	orange juice	mangoes

Student A: *I'd like some coffee.*
Student B: *I'd like some coffee and a bottle of water.*
Student C: *I'd like some coffee, a bottle of water, and three apples.*
Student D: *I'd like some coffee, a bottle of water, three apples, and . . .*

8a **Group Work** Divide the class into shoppers and vendors. Read your roles.

Shoppers

Work in pairs. Choose six things from the box in Exercise 7c and write your shopping list. You have $50 for all your shopping. Review the Audioscript on pages 138–139 and prepare to go shopping. Try to buy all your items. How much do you pay?

Vendors

1. Your teacher gives you a letter, A, B, C, or D.
   A: You sell fruit and vegetables.
   B: You sell drinks.
   C: You sell meat and fish.
   D: You sell dairy food (butter, milk, etc.).
2. Look at the box in Exercise 7c and the Unit Vocabulary on page 46 and find the correct type of food for your store. Choose four items and write a price next to each one (*water—$1 a bottle*). Then review the Audioscript on pages 138–139 and prepare to answer your customers' questions.

b When you finish, tell the class about the things you have.

Unit 4 Reference

Count and noncount nouns; *How much?/How many?*

Count nouns are things that can be counted. They have singular and plural forms and can have numbers in front of them.

> *one banana   three bananas*
> *twenty-five bananas*

Use *How many . . . ?* to ask questions about the number of count nouns.

> ***How many** bananas do you buy each week?*

Noncount nouns do not have plural forms and do not have numbers in front of them.

Use *How much . . . ?* to ask questions about the quantity of noncount nouns.

> ***How much** water do you drink every day?*

Show the quantity *(how much/many)* of count and noncount nouns by using another noun *(a bag)* or a measurement *(pounds)* + *of* in front of the noun.

> ***A bag** of bananas. **A pound** of bananas.*

a/an/some/any

Singular count nouns

Use *a/an* before singular count nouns. Use *a/an* in positive and negative statements and in questions.

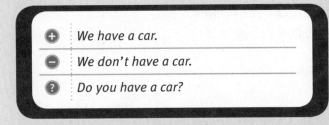

⊕	*We have a car.*
⊖	*We don't have a car.*
❓	*Do you have a car?*

Plural count and noncount nouns

If the number is unknown or not important, use *some* and *any* to talk about a number of something. Use *some* in positive statements and *any* in negative statements and questions. Use *some* and *any* with plural count and noncount nouns.

⊕	*We have some books/juice.*
⊖	*We don't have any books/juice.*
❓	*Do you have any books/juice?*

Object pronouns

Use subject pronouns (see page 11) before verbs and object pronouns after verbs.

Subject pronouns	*I*	Object pronouns	*me*
	he		*him*
	she		*her*
	it		*it*
	we		*us*
	you		*you*
	they		*them*

*He loves **her**.*

*He loves **them**.*

*She loves **him**.*

*They love **me**!*

Unit Vocabulary

Food

Dishes: burger   salad   hot dogs
fries   pizza   sandwich

Meat and fish: ham   lamb   chicken
(ground) beef   fish   pork   tuna
pepperoni

Dairy: butter   cheese   cream   ice cream   milk

Fruit and vegetables: papaya   pineapple
onion   grapes   mango   banana
melon   apple   tomato   strawberry
potato   carrot   lettuce

Drinks: coffee   soda   fruit/orange juice
tea   water   milk

Other: cereal   chips   cookies   pasta
rice   sugar   eggs   mayonnaise
bread (white/whole wheat)

Containers:
bag   bottle   box   can   carton   package

UNIT 5
Around the house

A

B

C

D

Warm Up

1a Match the rooms or places in the word box to each photo.

> ___ bathroom   ___ bedroom   ___ dining room   ___ garage
> ___ kitchen   ___ living room   ___ yard

b ▶ 1.45 Where can you do the activities below? Match the places in the box to the activities. Then listen and check.

1. cook _kitchen_____

2. take a shower _____

3. eat _____

4. sleep _____

5. park your car _____

6. watch TV _____

Reading

1 **Pair Work** Discuss. What kind of home do you live in? Do you like your home? Why or why not?

2a Look at the brochure and answer the questions.

   1. What is the purpose of this reading?

   _____

   2. What is unusual about these homes?

   _____

b Read the brochure and answer the questions.

   1. How many restaurants does the ship have?

   _____

   2. What do all the living rooms have?

   _____

   _____

The World of ResidenSea

Own a private luxury home ... at sea!

There are 110 luxury apartments on our ship *The World*, but that's not all! There are four restaurants, two swimming pools, and a gym. There are stores, but there aren't any factories or cars, so there's no city stress. All our apartments have a large living room (with dining area) and two or three bedrooms. Each bedroom has a private bathroom, and there's a stove, a refrigerator, a dishwasher, and a microwave in each fully equipped kitchen. Of course, there's no yard, but each apartment has a private balcony. All the living rooms have a widescreen TV, as well as DVD and CD players. Choose from four different styles for your sofas, chairs, beds, and other furniture, and make your apartment on the ship a very comfortable home.

—————— The World of ResidenSea ——————

Vocabulary | rooms and furniture

3 Look at the floor plan for one of the ResidenSea apartments. List the rooms (1–6) and the furniture (A–C).

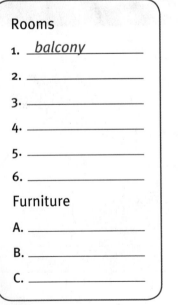

Rooms

1. *balcony*
2. _____
3. _____
4. _____
5. _____
6. _____

Furniture

A. _____
B. _____
C. _____

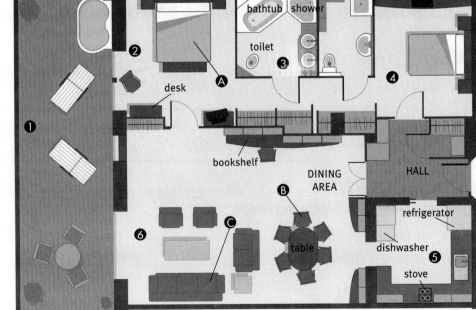

Grammar | *there is/there are*

4 Complete the Active Grammar box with *'s, is, isn't, are,* or *aren't.*

5 Look at the brochure and the floor plan on page 48 again. Complete the sentences with *'s, is, are, isn't,* or *aren't.*

1. There _____ some stores on the ship, but there _____ any cars.
2. _____ there any factories? No, there _____ .
3. There _____ a private balcony in each apartment.
4. _____ there a dining room? No, there _____ .

Active Grammar

	Singular	Plural
+	There's a gym. (There is)	There _____ 110 apartments.
−	There _____ a yard.	There _____ any cars.
?	_____ there a bookstore?	_____ there any restaurants?
	Yes, there is.	Yes, there _____ .
	No, there _____ .	No, there aren't.

See Reference page 56.

Listening

6 ▶1.46 Ryan Marshall wants to buy an apartment on the ship. Listen and answer the questions.

1. What is Ryan interested in? _____
2. Are there two-bedroom or three-bedroom apartments for sale? _____
3. Does Ryan think the apartment is expensive? _____
4. Do you think he has the money for the apartment? _____

Speaking

7 **SPEAKING EXCHANGE** Roleplay talking with a real estate agent.

Student A: Read the information on this page.
Student B: Look at the information on page 128.

Student A

You are interested in a house in the city. Student B has the details.

Ask questions to find out more about the house:

1. how big?
2. how many rooms?
3. what rooms?
4. yard/balcony?
5. where?
6. price?

Do you want to buy the house?

Now answer Student B's questions about the house on this page.

For Sale

beautiful country house
- 1,800 square feet
- three bedrooms, two bathrooms
- living room, dining room
- kitchen/breakfast area
- large front and back yards
- 15 miles from town

$240,000

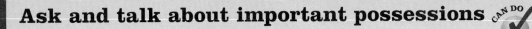

Listening

1a **Pair Work** Look at the four rooms. Which room(s) do you like? Why?

b **Pair Work** Look at the vocabulary on page 48. What's in the pictures? You have three minutes. Make a list of the things you can see.

Ex: *tables, stove, cell phone*

2a ▶1·47 Amanda Myers asks Pete Morgan some questions. Listen. Check (✓) the picture that shows Pete's apartment. ☐ A   ☐ B   ☐ C   ☐ D

b Listen again. Check (✓) the things Pete has and cross out (✗) the things he doesn't have.

☐ house	☐ yard	☐ balcony	☐ studio apartment
☐ stove	☐ sink	☐ microwave	☐ refrigerator
☐ chairs	☐ sofa	☐ diningroom table	☐ coffee table
☐ stereo	☐ TV	☐ cell phone	☐ laptop computer

Grammar | have/has

3a ▶1.48 Listen to the first part of the dialog again and complete the sentences.

Amanda: _____ (1.) you have your own place?

Pete: Yes, I _____ (2.). I _____ (3.) a studio apartment in the center of town.

Amanda: _____ (4.) it have a yard?

Pete: No, it _____ (5.) have a yard, but it _____ (6.) a small balcony.

b Look at the dialog and complete the Active Grammar box.

Active Grammar

➕	I/We/You/They	have	
	He/She/It	has	
➖	I/We/You/They	don't	*have*
	He/She/It	_____	
❓	_____	I/we/you/they	*have . . . ?*
	_____	he/she/it	
	Yes,	I/we/you/they	*do* .
	No,		_____ .
	Yes,	he/she/it	*does* .
	No,		*doesn't* .

See Reference page 56

Pronunciation | /æ/ and /ɑ/ sounds

4a ▶1.49 Listen to the underlined sounds. Which word's sound is not the same as the others? _____

He h<u>a</u>s a l<u>a</u>ptop, a c<u>a</u>t, and a w<u>a</u>tch.

b ▶1.50 Listen and check (✓) the word you hear.

1. ☐ hot ☐ hat   2. ☐ on ☐ an   3. ☐ top ☐ tap   4. ☐ pocket ☐ packet

Speaking

5 **Pair Work** Look at the four rooms again on page 50.

Student A: Choose one of the rooms, but don't tell your partner. Describe the things in the room. Use *there is/are* and *has*.

Student B: Listen to your partner. Ask questions. Which room is it?

6a Make a list of your family members and important personal possessions. Use the ideas in the box below.

> Family: husband, two children
> Home: two-bedroom apartment
> Furniture: desk, sofa, bed, diningroom table
> Electronics: CD player, computer
>
> Pets: cat
> Transportation: bicycle
> Other: watch

b **Pair Work** Find four things that:

• your partner has but you don't have.

• you have but your partner doesn't have.

> Do you have a car?

> No, I don't have a car, but I have a motorcycle.

Listening

1 Match these places to the five photos. Write the letters.

_____ mountain _____ beach _____ forest _____ city _____ lake

2 ▶ 1.51 Listen to five people talking about special places in their countries. Then listen again. Complete the chart.

Country	Place	Which Part?
1. *Mexico*	_____	_____
2. _____	_____	*east*
3. _____	*amazing forest*	_____
4. *South Korea*	_____	_____
5. _____	_____	*center*

3 **Pair Work** Take turns making sentences about the places with *there's* or *there are*.

> *In Mexico, there's a popular beach town in the west.*

Grammar | modifiers

4a ▶1.52 Listen and complete the sentences with *pretty*, *really*, *very*, or *not very*.

Ex: It's a ___really___ popular beach town.

1. The trees are _____ old.

2. It's tall and _____ beautiful.

3. It's _____ far from Kyoto.

b Write the correct modifiers next to the thermometer.

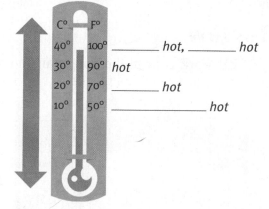

_____ hot, _____ hot

hot

_____ hot

_____ hot

See Reference page 56

Speaking

5a **Pair Work** Read the How To box. Then discuss these questions.

1. What is a special place in your country?

2. Where is it?

3. What's it like?

b **Group Work** Use your answers to talk about special places in your country.

One of my favorite places is . . .

How To:	
Describe where you live	
Say where you live	*I'm from . . . I live in . . .*
Describe places	*There are . . .* *In the south/north of . . .*
Give your opinion	*It's very modern.* *It's really beautiful.*

Reading and Writing

6 **Pair Work** Read the email on the right. Then ask and answer the questions.

Ex: Are there mountains in Australia?

Yes, there are. They're in the south.

1. What is there in the north of Australia?

2. Where are the deserts in Australia?

3. Where are the famous beaches?

7a Write an email to a friend about your country.

1. Look at your answers for Exercise 5a. What do you want to include in the email?

2. Write your email. Use *and* and *but* to join sentences. See page 133 for help.

b **Group Work** Read each other's emails. Suggest additional information if possible.

Hi Fran,

Thanks for your email. I'm so glad that you want to come to Australia. It's a very interesting country, with lots to see.

I come from Sydney, in the east of Australia. There are a lot of big cities in the east. But now I live in Perth, in the west. Perth is also a big city with lots of shops, and it's got some lovely squares. The Great Barrier Reef is in the north of the country, and there are some very nice beaches there. There are deserts in the centre, and in the east there are some long, wide rivers and famous beaches. We've also got mountains in the south.

You see, Australia is very good for holidays. I hope you can come this year!

Best wishes,

Monica

> Monica writes *centre* and *holidays*.
> In American English it is *center* and *vacations*.

Review

1 **Pair Work** Look at the floor plan and complete the dialog with *there is* or *there are*. Then practice with a partner.

A: Good morning. Can you give me some information about the apartment on Chandos Road?

B: Yes, of course. It's a very nice, big apartment. ___*There are*___ three bedrooms . . .

A: _____ (1.) a bathroom with each bedroom?

B: No, _____ (2.). The master bedroom has a bathroom, and then _____ (3.) one other bathroom in the apartment.

A: Is there a dining room?

B: No, _____ (4.) a dining room. But _____ (5.) a large living room with a dining area.

A: I know there's a yard, but _____ (6.) a deck?

B: No, _____ (7.), I'm afraid.

A: And finally, _____ (8.) a garage?

B: Yes, _____ (9.) a garage.

2 **Pair Work** Take turns asking questions and giving short answers.

Ex: Simon/sports car? No   *Does Simon have a sports car?*   *No, he doesn't.*

1. Rachel/a laptop computer? Yes
2. they/big house? No
3. your apartment/balcony? No

4. John/washing machine? Yes
5. you/cell phone? No
6. she/dining room? No

3 Complete the sentences with modifiers.

Ex: English is _*pretty*_ easy to learn.

1. My town/city is _____ beautiful.
2. People in my country are _____ friendly.
3. My country is _____ popular with tourists.

4. My diet is _____ healthy.
5. My home is _____ noisy.
6. My room is _____ large.

4 **Pair Work** List the items from the word box in the rooms where you usually find them. Some can go in more than one room.

lamp	armchair	bookshelves
TV	dishwasher	coffee table
sofa	stove	microwave
table	computer	refrigerator
bed	washing machine	

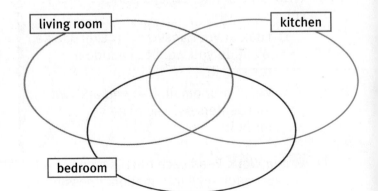

living room kitchen bedroom

Communication | talk about furnishing an apartment

5 **Pair Work** Look at the picture. What does the apartment have? What doesn't it have?

6a This is your new apartment. What do you think you need? Make a list of items.

b **Group Work** Work in groups of three. Compare your lists. Agree on ten important things and number them in order 1–10 (1 = very useful, 10 = not very useful).

NEW APARTMENT SHOPPING LIST

ITEM	SUPPLIER	COST
lamp		

7a **SPEAKING EXCHANGE** Work with the same group. You can buy things for your apartment, but you only have $1,000.

Talk about the things you want for your apartment, compare the prices, and complete the shopping list of the things you want to buy and the cost. Remember that you only have $1,000.

Student A: You have information from the Internet. Turn to page 128.

Student B: You have a catalog. Turn to page 131.

Student C: You have information from a local store. Look at the advertisement on this page.

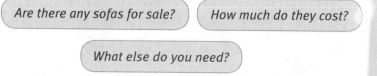

Are there any sofas for sale?   *How much do they cost?*

What else do you need?

Davis Electrical
Today's bargains!

Home theater
(DVD and flatscreen TV)
Only $600!

Combination
DVD player and TV
$225

Flatscreen TV
$400

Washing
machine
$330

Vacuum cleaner
$125

CD player
$195

Cordless phone and
answering machine
$130

Coffee maker
$50

b **Group Work** When you finish, compare your list with other groups.

Unit 5 Reference

there is/there are

	Singular	Plural
+	There's . . . (There is)	There are . . .
−	There isn't . . . (There is not)	There aren't . . . (There are not)
?	Is there . . . ?	Are there . . . ?
	Yes, there is./ No, there isn't.	Yes, there are./ No, there aren't.

Use *there is* (+ a singular noun) and *there are* (+ a plural noun) to talk about people or things for the first time. Use them to describe places.

Use *there's*, *there isn't*, and *there aren't* when you speak.
> There's a huge forest in the west.

Use *There's*, not *There are*, to introduce a list of singular objects.
> There's a swimming pool, a lake, and a restaurant at the hotel.

have/has

	I/We/You/They	He/She/It
+	have	has
−	don't have	doesn't have
?	Do . . . have?	Does . . . have?
	Yes, we do. No, I don't.	Yes, it does. No, she doesn't.

Modifiers: very/pretty/really

The words *(not) very*, *pretty*, and *really* are modifiers. Put them in front of an adjective to make it stronger or weaker.

Use *very* and *really* to make the adjective stronger.

Use *pretty* and *not very* to make the adjective weaker.
> This car is **very/really** expensive!
> This car is **pretty** expensive.
> This car isn't **very** expensive.

Adjectives and places

Use adjectives to describe nouns.
> a hot, dry desert
> a long, wide river
> a large lake
> a beautiful beach
> an amazing forest
> a popular beach town

Adjectives are usually placed in front of the noun. Put a comma between two adjectives in front of a noun.

Unit Vocabulary

Types of home

apartment	house
townhouse	studio apartment

Rooms and parts of a house

hall	balcony	bathroom
deck	kitchen	dining room
yard	bedroom	living room
garage		

Furniture

bed	table	bookshelves
desk	chair	coffee table
sofa	armchair	
diningroom chairs/table		

Equipment and possessions

bath	shower	microwave
sink	CD player	dishwasher
video	DVD player	refrigerator
stove	coffee maker	
toilet	vacuum cleaner	
stereo	washing machine	
answering machine		

Warm Up

1a Circle the places in the word box that you see in the photos.

library	bank	museum	café	factory	church
art gallery	movie theater	bookstore	newsstand	phone store	police station
post office	restaurant	school	hospital	supermarket	train station

b ▶1.53 Listen to the words from Exercise 1a. How many syllables does each word have? Practice saying them.
Ex: *art/gal/le/ry – 4   bank – 1*

American English	British English
bookstore	bookshop
movie theater	cinema
newsstand	newsagent's

c **Pair Work** What can you do at these places? Discuss.

What can you do at a bookstore?   *You can buy books at a bookstore.*

Talk about your past

CAN DO ✓

Recycled **buildings**

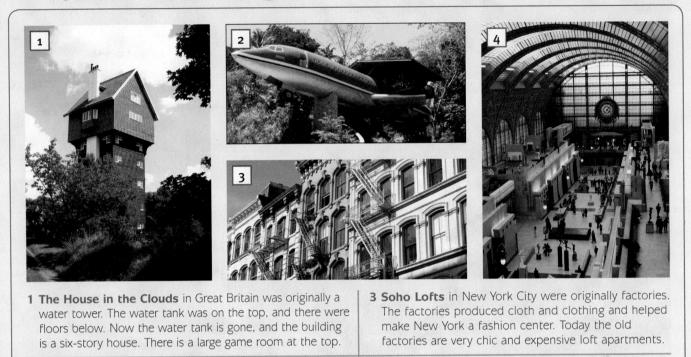

1 The House in the Clouds in Great Britain was originally a water tower. The water tank was on the top, and there were floors below. Now the water tank is gone, and the building is a six-story house. There is a large game room at the top.

2 The 727 Suite in Costa Rica was a working airplane. At the end of its flying career, resort owners noticed it at the San Jose airport. Trucks carried the plane into the jungle in Manuel Antonio. It is now a two-bedroom hotel suite with beautiful ocean views.

3 Soho Lofts in New York City were originally factories. The factories produced cloth and clothing and helped make New York a fashion center. Today the old factories are very chic and expensive loft apartments.

4 The Musée d'Orsay in Paris was once a busy train station. But its platforms were too short for newer, longer trains. In 1971, the French government planned to tear down the station. But many people loved the building. It is now an art museum.

Reading

1a **Pair Work** What are the buildings in the photos? Read the descriptions and check your answers.

b Match the buildings with *In the past* and *Now*.

	In the past	**Now**
1. The House in the Clouds	factories	a hotel suite
2. The 727 Suite	a water tower	an art museum
3. Soho Lofts	a train station	apartments
4. The Musée d'Orsay	an airplane	a house

Grammar | simple past of *be*

2a Complete the Active Grammar box with *was, were, wasn't,* or *weren't.*

b **Pair Work** Make two sentences about each building using the past and present of *be*.

    Ex: *The House in the Clouds was a water tower. Now it is a house.*

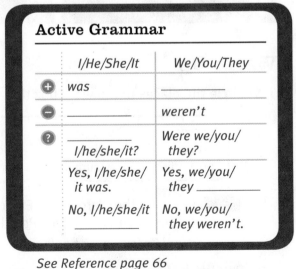

Active Grammar

	I/He/She/It	*We/You/They*
➕	was	_____
➖	_____	weren't
❓	_____ I/he/she/it?	Were we/you/they?
	Yes, I/he/she/it was.	Yes, we/you/they _____
	No, I/he/she/it _____	No, we/you/they weren't.

See Reference page 66

Speaking

3 **Pair Work** Look at the phrases in the box. Where were you at these times?

> ~~six hours ago~~   ten minutes ago   last Saturday evening   at 8:00 last night
> an hour ago   yesterday at noon   last Sunday afternoon

> Where were you six hours ago?   I was at home.   Were you in the living room?   No, I wasn't. I was in bed.

Grammar | simple past of regular verbs

4a Find the simple past of these verbs in the descriptions on page 58.

1. notice _____   2. help _____   3. carry _____   4. plan _____

b Write the verbs in Exercise 4a next to the simple past endings.

1. + -ed _____   3. + n + -ed _____
2. – -y + -ied _____   4. + -d _____

See Reference page 66

5 **Pair Work** Take turns making sentences in the simple past from the cues.

  Ex: My wife/work/in the San Carlos hospital   *My wife worked in the San Carlos hospital.*

1. I /move/to Florida in 2010
2. Alicia/study/at the Sorbonne
3. My brother/start/a new job yesterday
4. You/marry/my father in 1977
5. We/look/for a new apartment last year
6. My mother/plan/the vacation

Pronunciation | simple past endings

6a ▶1·54 Listen to the simple past endings of these verbs. Do they all sound the same? _____

  /t/ work*ed*   /d/ open*ed*   /ɪd/ decid*ed*

b ▶1·55 Listen and write the verbs in the correct column. Then repeat them.

> visited   finished   lived   changed   started   looked   produced   planned   studied

/t/ worked	/d/ opened	/ɪd/ decided

c **Pair Work** Read the sentences in Exercise 5. Ask your partner to check your pronunciation.

Speaking

7 **Pair Work** Make notes about your past. Then tell your partner about your life.

> *When I was a child, we lived in Osaka, but we moved to Tokyo in 2005.*

Reading

1 Read the article and answer the questions.

   1. How many hours was Robin Andrews away from home?

   _____

   2. What does *missing* mean?

   _____

   3. Why was Robin confused?

   _____

2 ▶1.56 Listen to an interview with Robin. There are some mistakes in the interviewer's notes for her article. Listen and correct the <u>underlined</u> phrases.

   1. Robin disappeared <u>at 3:30</u>.

   2. He walked <u>three</u> miles to town.

   3. He stopped by <u>the library</u>.

   4. He wanted to go <u>shopping</u>.

   5. <u>A young man</u> helped him.

   6. <u>His mother</u> picked him up.

Man was missing for 16 hours

Robin Andrews, 24, of Scarsdale, New York, was missing for 16 hours last Tuesday. Mr. Andrews disappeared at 2:30 in the afternoon when he walked out of the house to get some things downtown. In town, two miles from his home, Mr. Andrews got some money from an ATM and stopped by the post office, but he doesn't remember anything after that. Mr. Andrews is very confused. "I wanted to go to a cafe, but something strange happened." It seems that Mr. Andrews arrived in Hartsdale, two miles from Scarsdale.

Vocabulary | prepositions of location

3 Write the correct preposition under each illustration: *on, in front of, under, between, in, behind,* or *next to.*

Grammar | simple past: regular/questions/short answers

4a Read the questions in the Active Grammar box. Circle the correct words to complete the rule.

b **Pair Work** Ask and answer questions for the sentences in Exercise 2. Use these question words.

> What time?   How many?   Where?   Who?

> *What time did Robin disappear?*

Active Grammar

1. *Did you get lost?*

2. *Where did you go then?*

To make questions in the simple past, use <u>do</u> / <u>did</u> and the <u>past form</u> / <u>base form</u> of the verb.

See Reference page 66

5a **SPEAKING EXCHANGE** What happened to Robin? Tell your partner your story and decide which ending you like best.

Student A: Look at page 128.   Student B: Look at page 131.

b ▶1.57 Listen. Which story is correct?

Speaking

6 **Pair Work** Ask and answer questions. Find out what your partner did:

> yesterday   last night   last weekend   on their last vacation

You can ask only ten *yes/no* questions.

> Did you watch TV last night?   No, I didn't.

Listening

7a ▶1.58 Listen. You are at the library. Follow the directions on the map. Write the letters of these places.

_____ post office

_____ bookstore

_____ bus station

b Listen again and read the expressions in the How To box.

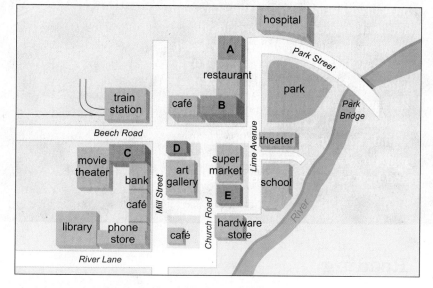

How To:	
Ask for and give directions	
Ask for directions	*Can you tell me how to get to the bank?*
	(Excuse me,) do you know the way to the bus station?
Give directions	*Turn left at the next street.*
	Then go straight.
	Take a right onto Beech Road.
	Go down one block. It's on the left/right.

8 **Pair Work** Use the map. Ask for and give directions.

From	To
the bank	the bridge
the bus station	the train station
the library	the theater
the hospital	the art gallery

People always need to answer the question "Where am I?" when they travel. Ancient people used the <u>stars</u> to navigate. But of course this system of navigation didn't work during the day. In the 12th century sailors invented the <u>compass</u>—this shows north, south, east and west, and it works at day or night. In the 18th and 19th centuries, there were many new inventions, including the <u>sextant</u>. This measured the position of the stars and sun and showed your approximate location, but it didn't show your exact location. Everything changed in 1973 when the United States launched the 24 <u>satellites</u> of the Global Positioning System (GPS). Computers combine the signals from the GPS satellites with <u>maps</u> to show exactly where you are and how to get to another place.

Reading

1a Read the article quickly. Circle the best title.

What is GPS?   How Ancient People Traveled   Navigation Past and Present

b Read the article again. Match the <u>underlined</u> words in the article to the pictures below.

| A | B | C | D | E |

_____   _____   _____   _____   _____

c Look for these words in the article and match them to their meanings.

1. navigate   a. not exact
2. approximate   b. the place or position of something
3. location   c. find your position or direction when you travel
4. signal   d. electronic communication between machines

Grammar | simple past: negative

2a Read the sentence in the Active Grammar box. Circle the correct words to complete the rule.

b **Pair Work** Correct these false statements.

Ex: Ancient people ~~used~~ compasses.   *didn't use*

1. The sextant showed exact location.
2. People used cars in the 16ᵗʰ century.
3. Leonardo da Vinci invented the compass.
4. Marco Polo owned a cell phone.

> ### Active Grammar
>
> *This system of navigation didn't work during the day.*
>
> To make negative statements in the simple past, use <u>don't</u> / <u>didn't</u> and the <u>past form</u> / <u>base form</u> of the verb.

See Reference page 66

Vocabulary | transportation

3 Match the forms of transportation to the famous places.

Transportation	Places
_____ 1. red buses	a. Japan
_____ 2. yellow taxis	b. London
_____ 3. water buses	c. San Francisco
_____ 4. high-speed trains	d. Amsterdam
_____ 5. cable cars	e. Venice
_____ 6. bicycles	f. New York

Speaking

4 **Pair Work** Discuss.

1. How do you get around your town/city (by car/bus, on foot, etc.)?
2. Which form of transportation do you like best?

Writing

5a Read the paragraph. <u>Underline</u> all the verbs in the simple past.

I visited Bangkok last year with my friend, Jenny. We liked the food, but we didn't like the weather—it was very hot! We stayed in a hotel near the river. There were lots of tourists there, and we talked to some people from Australia. The city is huge, so we didn't walk very much. We traveled on the new overhead railway. It was very fast and comfortable. We looked at lots of temples and we watched the boats on the river. We wanted some souvenirs, so we visited the fantastic street markets . . .

b Write a paragraph about your last vacation. Use the <u>underlined</u> verbs from Exercise 5a.

Review

1 Write the simple past form of the verbs in the correct column.

carry	change	close	decide
finish	jog	look	live
marry	move	own	plan
start	stop	want	worry

+ -ed	+ -d	- -y + -ied	+ consonant + -ed
finished	changed	carried	jogged

2 **Pair Work** Take turns asking and answering simple past questions with the cues.

Ex: Albert Einstein/understand/mathematics? (✓)

Did Albert Einstein understand mathematics?

Yes, he did.

Ex: Charles Darwin/French? (✗ British)

Was Charles Darwin French?

No, he wasn't. He was British.

1. Pablo Picasso/Spanish? (✓)
2. Mozart /play/the guitar? (✗ the piano)
3. President Kennedy/Russian? (✗ American)
4. the US/launch/GPS satellites in 1983? (✗ 1973)
5. Alexander Graham Bell/invent/the computer? (✗ the telephone)
6. the ancient Romans/speak Latin? (✓)
7. Neil Armstrong/walk/on Mars? (✗ the Moon)

3 Complete the paragraph with prepositions of place.

Alan's room is really messy! There's an armchair in the room, but there are some shoes ___on___ it, and there's a plant _____ (1.) it. There's a phone and some credit cards _____ (2.) the bed, and there are CDs and books _____ (3.) it. There's a cup of cold coffee _____ (4.) the bed. There's a newspaper _____ (5.) the sink. His suitcase is on the floor, open, _____ (6.) the desk and the sink, and his laptop is _____ (7.) the suitcase.

4 **Pair Work** What are two places where you can do these things? Tell your partner.

1. have something to eat or drink
2. buy things to take home
3. look at paintings
4. begin a trip
5. sit for a few minutes
6. ask people for help

You can have something to eat or drink at a restaurant or a café.

Communication |
understand a directory and ask for things in stores

5 **Group Work** Discuss.

1. What do you see in the photo?

2. Do you shop at department stores? Which ones?

3. Why are department stores useful?

4. How do people move from one floor to another?

6a ▶1·59 Listen to customers asking for information in a department store. Complete the directory.

STORE DIRECTORY	
Fifth floor	_____ • beds • rugs • luggage
Fourth floor	china • crystal • _____ • silver
Third floor	men's clothing • _____ • men's accessories
Second floor	women's clothing • women's shoes • children and infants
First floor	cosmetics • perfumes • _____ • accessories
Lower Level	gourmet foods • _____ • restaurant

b Listen again. Then read the How To box.

How To:	
Ask for what you want in a store	
Ask where something is	*Where can I find men's shoes?*
	I'm looking for a necklace.
	Where are the escalators/elevators?
Ask for something	*Do you have a store directory?*

c **Pair Work** Ask and answer questions about where to find things. Use the information in the store directory.

> ~~sofas~~   women's jeans   chocolates   men's belts   suitcases   dresses
> dishes   baking pans   eye shadow   baby clothes   earrings   something to eat

Can I help you?   *Where can I find sofas?*   *They're in the furniture department on the fifth floor.*

Unit 6 Reference

Simple past

Use the simple past to talk about actions and situations in the past. The actions and situations are finished.

> My hair **was** red when I was a girl, but it's gray now.

be

⊕	I/He/She/It was	We/You/They were
⊖	I/He/She/It wasn't (was not)	We/You/They weren't (were not)
?	Was I/he/she/it?	Were we/you/they?
	Yes, I/he/she/it was.	Yes, we/you/they were.
	No, I/he/she/it wasn't.	No, we/you/they weren't.

> She **was** tired last night.
> They **weren't** at the theater yesterday.
> Was Karen at the office? No, she **wasn't**.
> **Were** the musicians good? Yes, they **were**.

Regular verbs: positive

Make the simple past of most regular verbs by adding *-ed* to the verb.

> work → work**ed**, watch → watch**ed**,
> listen → listen**ed**

Note the spelling rules:

- add *-d* to verbs that end in *-e*
  live → liv**ed**, chang**e** → chang**ed**
- with verbs that end in consonant + *-y*, change *-y* to *-i* and add *-ed*
  study → stud**ied**, carry → carr**ied**
  (If the verb ends in vowel + *-y*, add *-ed*:
  stay → stay**ed**.)
- with verbs of one syllable that end in vowel + consonant, double the consonant and add *-ed*
  plan → plan**ned**, jog → jog**ged**

Negative

Did + *not* + base form of verb

> Ancient people **did not use** compasses.
> People **didn't know** their exact location.

Questions

Wh- questions

Wh-word + *did* + subject pronoun + base form of verb

> When did you **finish** work yesterday?

Yes/no questions

Did + subject pronoun + base form of verb

> **Did** you **study** in college? Yes, I **did**.

Prepositions of place

The books are **in** the bookshelf. The picture is **on** the bookshelf. The waste basket is **under** the desk. The chair is **in front of** the desk. The map is **behind** the desk. The desk is **next to** the bookshelf. The plant is **between** the bookshelf and the desk.

The preposition *at* can mean *in* or *near*.

> I'm at the phone shop. (in/in front of)
> I'm at the door. (next to/in front of)

We also use *at* with a very general meaning.

> I'm at home. Are you at work?

Unit Vocabulary

Places in a town

ATM	factory	art gallery
café	hospital	bus station
bank	museum	movie theater
park	bookstore	train station
bridge	restaurant	post office
church	newsstand	police station
school	phone store	department store
library	supermarket	

Forms of transportation

bicycle	boat	bus	cable car
car	taxi	train	water bus

UNIT 7
Describing people

Warm Up

1a Complete the descriptions of the people in the photos with A–G.

1. _G_ is young.
2. ____ has blue eyes.
3. ____ has blonde hair.
4. ____ wears glasses.
5. ____ has gray hair.
6. ____ has a beard.
7. ____ has long black hair.

b ▶2.02 Listen and compare your answers.

2 **Pair Work** Describe and identify people.
   Student A: Describe a person from the photos.
   Student B: Point at the person.

This person has black hair and wears glasses.

Write an informal letter describing family members

GRAMMAR pronouns: *one/ones*

Dear Carol,

A Thanks for your letter about my old friends in New Zealand!

B Everything is fine here. I arrived in Rio de Janeiro a month ago to start my course, and then I moved in with my host family. They live in a big flat near the beach in Ipanema.

C The family is very nice. Mr. and Mrs. Silva are middle-aged and very friendly. They have three children. Tina is my age. She has dark hair and she's pretty. She's tall, like me. João is the middle one; he's 15. He's short and he's very tan from playing football! Carlos is the young one, and he's a bit heavy. He's cute, and he laughs all the time.

D Every morning I go to college. The classes are tiring, especially the literature ones. I usually go to the beach in the afternoon. The beach here is beautiful and the sea is warm. There is a really handsome man on the beach. I think he's nice, but I'm pretty shy so I don't talk to him!

E Write to me soon and tell me all your news.

Love,

Marianne

Marianne writes *flat*.
In American English, it's *apartment*.

Reading and Vocabulary | descriptive adjectives

1a **Pair Work** Marianne is 22. She is from New Zealand but is going to college in Brazil. Read the letter. Then ask and answer the questions with a partner.

1. What did Marianne do a month ago?
2. Where does she live?
3. How many people are in her host family?
4. What does she do in the morning?
5. What does she do in the afternoon?
6. Who does she see on the beach?

b Read the letter again. Match the people and the adjectives.

1. Mr. and Mrs. Silva   a. tan, short
2. Tina   b. handsome, nice
3. João   c. friendly, middle-aged
4. Carlos   d. dark hair, pretty
5. the man on the beach   e. tall, shy
6. Marianne   f. young, heavy

2a Look for adjectives in Exercise 1b with the opposite meanings.

Ex: ugly _pretty, handsome_

1. slim _____   3. mean _____
2. old _____   4. tall _____

b **Pair Work** Put the adjectives from Exercises 1b and 2a in the correct columns. Which adjectives can go in more than one column?

Body	Face	Hair	Height	Age	Personality

3 **Pair Work** Think of someone in your class or a famous person. Describe him or her to your partner, but don't say his or her name. Can your partner guess the person?

> She's an actor from Mexico. She's short and has dark hair . . .

> Do you mean Salma Hayek?

Grammar | pronouns: *one/ones*

4a Read the sentences in the Active Grammar box and write the meaning for the underlined words.

> **Active Grammar**
>
> 1. *They have three children. João is the middle <u>one</u>.* _____
> 2. *The classes are tiring, especially the literature <u>ones</u>.* _____
>
> **Meanings**
>
> classes   class   student   child

See Reference page 76

b Read the paragraph. Find four more words you can change to *one* (or *ones*).

> When I was a child I lived in three different houses. The first house *one* was beautiful. The second house was pretty small, but it was in a nice location. The third house wasn't very nice, but there were six bedrooms. I used the bedroom on the second floor. The other bedrooms were on the first floor.

Writing

5a Match the statements to paragraphs A–E in Marianne's letter in Exercise 1.

_C_ 1. Marianne describes her host family.
____ 2. She asks Carol to do something.
____ 3. She thanks Carol.
____ 4. She says what she does.
____ 5. She says where she lives.

How To:	
Start and finish informal letters	
Start	*Dear* + first name
Finish	*Love,* + your name (for close friends/family)
	Yours, + your name (for others)

b Read the How To box.

c Your family is a host family for foreign students. Sue, an American, wants to stay with you. Write a letter and tell her about where you live and your family.

Listening

1a Jane Birch has a lot of friends. Match their names to the photos.

_____ 1. Mrs. Suzuki wears glasses.

_____ 2. David is young and has brown hair.

_____ 3. Tara is tall and slim.

_____ 4. Alberto has a beard.

_____ 5. Mr. Suzuki is bald.

b **Pair Work** Add information to the descriptions in Exercise 1a.

> _Mrs. Suzuki has black hair. She likes to read._

2a Jane has some presents for her friends. Match the words to the items in the picture (A–G).

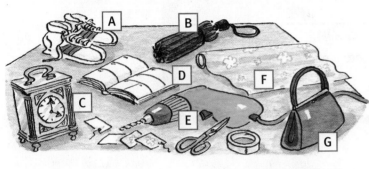

_____ clock   _____ electric drill
_____ purse   _____ datebook
_A_ sneakers   _____ wrapping paper
_____ umbrella

b **Pair Work** Who are the presents for? Discuss. Give reasons for your guesses.

> _I think the purse is for Tara because . . ._

c ▶2.03 Jane went to work this morning. Her husband Mike called and asked her about the presents. Listen and check your answers for Exercise 2b.

A. _David_   E. _____
B. _____   F. _____
C. _____   G. _____
D. _____

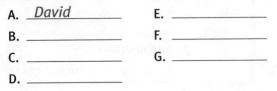

Grammar | possessive pronouns

3a Read the Audioscript on page 140 and complete the Active Grammar box.

b **Pair Work** Take turns rephrasing the sentences. Use a possessive pronoun (and a verb if needed) to replace the phrases underlined.

> **Ex:** These aren't my CDs; they <u>belong to Jane</u>.

> *These aren't my CDs; they're hers.*

1. Excuse me. Is this <u>your bag</u>?
2. Use the blue pen; the red one <u>belongs to me</u>.
3. Are these sandwiches <u>for us</u>?
4. That wasn't her phone number; it was <u>John's</u>.
5. The house next to the church <u>belonged to them</u>.

Active Grammar

Possessive adjectives	Possessive pronouns
my	_____
his	_____
her	_____
its	*its*
our	_____
your	_____
their	_____

See Reference page 76

Pronunciation | /θ/ sound

4a ▶2.04 Listen to the *th* sound /θ/ in the word *bir<u>th</u>day*. Is it the same as the sound in *bro<u>th</u>er* or *ba<u>th</u>room*? _____

b ▶2.05 Listen and circle the words you hear.

1. sick thick   2. sink think   3. free three   4. first thirst   5. tree three

Vocabulary | ordinal numbers/months

5a Complete the chart with ordinal numbers in the word box.

> thirtieth   tenth   twelfth   twenty-third   thirteenth   fifth   sixth
> eleventh   third   seventh   thirty-first   twentieth   first   ninth   fifteenth

1. _____	5. _____	9. _____	13. _____	22. *twenty-second*
2. *second*	6. _____	10. _____	14. *fourteenth*	23. _____
3. _____	7. _____	11. _____	15. _____	30. _____
4. *fourth*	8. *eighth*	12. _____	20. _____	31. _____

b ▶2.06 Listen and check your answers. Then repeat.

6a Number the months 1–12 in the correct order.

b **Group Work** Find students with:

1. a birthday in the same month as yours.
2. the first and last birthdays of the year.
3. a birthday this month.
4. a birthday next month.
5. a birthday last month.

Litter Changes Woman's Life

1 March 29th of last year started out as a usual day for Jan Lowry. She got up, had breakfast, and left her apartment for work. On the sidewalk outside her door, she saw a piece of litter. She decided to pick it up and throw it away at the subway station. It was a lottery ticket with the numbers 44-67-99-81 on it. "Somebody lost the lottery," she thought. She put the ticket in her coat pocket and forgot about it. When she got home that evening, she felt something in her pocket. She took the ticket out of her pocket and then threw it away.

2 After dinner, Ms. Lowry turned on the TV. She was flipping channels when she heard the numbers "44-67-99-81." She went to the garbage, got the lottery ticket, and checked the lottery site on the Internet. She suddenly felt funny and fell to the floor. She had the winning ticket—worth $50 million.

3 After she won the money, hundreds of people called and told Ms. Lowry the ticket was theirs. She didn't believe them. She changed her name and took a long vacation. She then bought houses in Paris and New York and gave away a large amount of money, but she still has enough to live well for the rest of her life. She is still a neat-freak, and picks up litter whenever she sees it.

Reading

1 Read the article. How did litter change a woman's life? _____

2 Look for words in the article with these meanings.

(paragraph 1) put in the garbage _____ (paragraph 2) changing _____

(paragraph 3) very clean and organized person _____

3 Put the events in the correct order. Number them 1–6.

_____ She found the ticket in her coat and threw it away.

_____ She put the ticket in her pocket.

_____ She changed her name, took a vacation, and bought houses.

_____ She heard the winning lottery numbers on the TV and got the ticket.

_____ Ms. Lowry picked up a piece of litter on the sidewalk.

_____ People called to tell her the ticket was theirs.

4 **Pair Work** Ask and answer the questions.

1. When did Ms. Lowry find the ticket?
2. Why did Ms. Lowry pick it up?
3. How did Ms. Lowry find out she had the winning ticket?
4. How much money did Ms. Lowry win?
5. How many people called her?
6. How did she spend some of the money?

5 Look at Exercises 1–4 and match the strategies to each exercise.

_____ 1. Understand the main idea   _____ 3. Figure out new words

_____ 2. Identify the main events   _____ 4. Understand details

Grammar | simple past: irregular verbs

6a Complete the Active Grammar box. Look at the article on page 72 again. Find the past forms of these irregular verbs.

b **Pair Work** Take turns making simple past sentences with these cues.

> Ex: I / go / to the gym after class.

> I went to the gym after class.

1. I / take / a one-week vacation.
2. He / buy / a new sofa.
3. They / go / shopping at the mall.
4. My husband / get / a raise at work.
5. We / have / dinner at a new restaurant.

Active Grammar

1. buy _____
2. fall _____
3. feel _____
4. forget _____
5. get _____
6. give _____
7. go _____
8. have _____
9. hear _____
10. leave _____
11. put _____
12. see _____
13. think _____
14. throw _____
15. win _____

See Reference page 76

Speaking

7a Write five sentences about yourself. Use the time phrases in the word box.

> yesterday   last weekend   last month   six months ago   last year

> I saw an interesting movie on TV yesterday.

b **Pair Work** Ask and answer questions about the five sentences.

> What did you do yesterday?   I saw an interesting movie on TV.   What did you see?

8a Find the simple past forms of these verbs on page 136. Make five *wh-* questions with these words.

meet go shopping have drive leave spend speak take give buy feel make write go to bed understand come

> What did you buy last week?   Who did you go shopping with?

b **Pair Work** Ask and answer the questions.

Review

1 Read the dialog. Find seven words you can change to *one* or *ones*. Then practice with a partner.

    Ex: A: There are so many ~~sofas~~ here, Philip. Which sofas do you like?   *ones*

          B: Well, I like the brown ~~sofa~~.   *one*

    1. A: No, it's ugly. What about the red sofa?

    2. B: It's OK. Now, chairs. Do you like modern chairs?

    3. A: Yes. I like the chairs in the corner.

    4. B: The metal chairs? Yes, they're nice. But how about this chair?

    5. A: No, I don't like that chair.

    6. B: Well, I don't like this store. Let's go to a different store.

2 Match questions on the left to questions on the right with the same meaning. Share your answers with a partner.

    1. Does this bag belong to you?   a. Are these ours?

    2. Is this his?   b. Is this hers?

    3. Is this Mary's DVD player?   c. Is this mine?

    4. Are these our letters?   d. Do these books belong to them?

    5. Are these theirs?   e. Is this yours?

    6. Is this present for me?   f. Is this ours?

    7. Are these mine or yours?   g. Are these my keys or your keys?

    8. Does this umbrella belong to us?   h. Does this belong to Mr. McBride?

3 Complete the article with the correct simple past form of the verbs in parentheses.

Robert Atkins, famous for the Atkins Diet, died at age 72 after a fall in the street. Atkins, a doctor, studied at the University of Michigan. He _____ (1. become) quite fat after he finished college and he tried different diets to lose weight. He _____ (2. think) that people _____ (3. have) problems with weight because they _____ (4. eat) the wrong things, and he _____ (5. write) his first diet book in 1970. Not many people _____ (6. buy) the book at first, but Atkins's diet is now very popular, and his books are bestsellers.

4 Complete the sentences with ordinal numbers. Share your answers with a partner.

      1   ~~16~~   8   18   25

    Ex: Abraham Lincoln was the _*sixteenth*_ president of the United States.

    1. August is the _____ month of the year.

    2. Christmas Day is on the _____ of December.

    3. Neil Armstrong was the _____ man on the Moon.

    4. US citizens can vote after their _____ birthday.

Communication | identify a person from a simple description

5a ▶ 2.07 Listen. Why is the young man at the police station? _____

b Listen again and complete the missing person form.

c Which picture shows the missing woman? _____

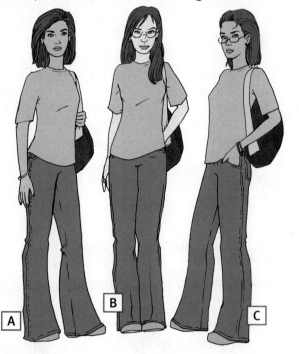

A   B   C

<table>
<tr><td colspan="2">MISSING PERSON FORM</td></tr>
</table>

Name: _____

Man ☐ Woman ☐ Age: _____

Height: _____

Hair: _____

Body type: _____

Eyes: _____

Skin: _____

Other features: _____

_____

Last seen: _____

Name of person reporting: *Scott Kennedy*

Relationship to missing person: _____

6 **Pair Work** Look at the Audioscript on page 140. Underline the questions. Then practice the dialog with a partner.

MISSING PERSON FORM

Name: _____

Man ☐ Woman ☐ Age: _____

Height: _____

Hair: _____

Body type: _____

Eyes: _____

Skin: _____

Other features: _____

_____

Last seen: _____

Name of person reporting: _____

Relationship to missing person: _____

7a **SPEAKING EXCHANGE** Ask and answer questions about a missing person with a partner.

Student A: Your friend is missing. You are at the police station. Turn to page 129 and choose one of the people. Decide the relationship of the person to you and when and how they disappeared.

Student B: You are a police officer. Complete the form. Ask your partner questions and find out about the missing person. (You can use the underlined questions in the Audioscript on page 140 to help you.) Then turn to page 129 and identify the person.

> *Excuse me, I want to report a missing person.*

> *When did you last see the person?*

b **Pair Work** Change roles and repeat. This time use the pictures on page 132.

Unit 7 Reference

Pronouns: *one/ones*

Use *one* or *ones* to avoid repeating a noun. Use *one* after *this*, *that*, or an adjective.

A: *Do you want the black **pen** or the blue **one**?*

B: *The blue **one**.*

Use *ones* to replace plural nouns. Use *ones* after *these*, *those*, or an adjective.

A: *Did you buy the brown **shoes** or the black **ones**?*

B: *I bought the black **ones**.*

Possessive pronouns

Possessive pronouns show the person that something is for or who it belongs to. Use them in place of a possessive adjective and a noun.

*This is **my coat**. = This is **mine**.*

Subject pronoun	Possessive adjectives	Possessive pronouns
I	*my*	*mine*
he	*his*	*his*
she	*her*	*hers*
it	*its*	*its*
we	*our*	*ours*
you	*your*	*yours*
they	*their*	*theirs*

Simple past: irregular verbs

(See also page 66)

Many common verbs in English have an irregular past form; they do not end in *-ed* in the past.

have → *had*   *do* → *did*   *go* → *went*
make → *made*

See page 136 for a list of irregular simple past forms.

These verbs are irregular only in the affirmative. They form the negative and questions with *did* and the base form, like regular verbs.

*He **went** to Australia on vacation last year.*

*He **didn't go** to Australia on vacation last year.*

***Did** he **go** to Australia on vacation last year?*

Ordinal numbers

Use these numbers with nouns to talk about dates.

*My **first** child was a boy.*

*the **third** of September/September the **third***

Dates can be written in different ways.

September 3   September 3rd

1.	first	18.	eighteenth
2.	second	19.	nineteenth
3.	third	20.	twentieth
4.	fourth	21.	twenty-first
5.	fifth	22.	twenty-second
6.	sixth	23.	twenty-third
7.	seventh	24.	twenty-fourth
8.	eighth	30.	thirtieth
9.	ninth	31.	thirty-first
10.	tenth	40.	fortieth
11.	eleventh	50.	fiftieth
12.	twelfth	60.	sixtieth
13.	thirteenth	70.	seventieth
14.	fourteenth	80.	eightieth
15.	fifteenth	90.	ninetieth
16.	sixteenth	100.	one hundredth
17.	seventeenth		

Ordinal numbers are often written like this:

*first = 1st   second = 2nd   third = 3rd
fourth = 4th   fifth = 5th, etc.*

Unit Vocabulary

Describing words
Adjectives:

Body	Face	Skin	Hair	
slim	pretty	dark	dark	black
heavy	handsome	fair	bald*	blonde
	ugly	tan	short	gray

Height	Age	Personality
tall	middle-aged	nice
short	young	friendly
	old	shy
		mean

Nouns: glasses   beard

---

*We say *He's bald*, not ~~He has bald hair.~~

UNIT 8
Dressing right

Warm Up

1   **Pair Work** Answer the questions about the photos.

   1. Where are the people and what are they doing?

   2. What are the seasons? (spring, summer, fall, winter)

2a Look for these clothing items in the photos. Which photo are they in? Write A–D.

   _____ coat   _____ hat   _____ jacket   _____ jeans

   ___*A*___ scarf   _____ shorts   _____ T-shirt   _____ boots

  b Name other clothes that you see in the photos. _____

Write a request to a colleague CAN DO ✓

GRAMMAR adverbs: frequency

Reading

1a Read the advice column quickly and match the letters (1–3) to the answers (A–C).

Letter 1. _____   Letter 2. _____   Letter 3. _____

b Read the column again and list the problems and solutions.

Ex: *Problem = cold when leave, cool on plane, but hot when arrive   Solution = layers*

Problem = _____   Solution = _____

Problem = _____   Solution = _____

WHAT TO WEAR?
Alison Bering answers all your clothes questions.

1 Dear Alison,
Can you give us some advice? We usually go to the Caribbean with our three young children in December. It's always really cold when we leave home, it's cool on the plane, but it's hot and sunny when we arrive—it's really difficult with children! So, what clothes can we all wear?   Mr. and Mrs. Jackson

2 Dear Alison,
I work for an international bank and I wear a suit and tie all the time for work. I often travel for business and I am never comfortable on the plane in my formal clothes. Can you suggest anything?
Geoffrey W.

3 Dear Alison,
I'm 22. I love casual clothes and I usually wear sneakers, a T-shirt, and jeans. I hardly ever wear skirts, and I hate dresses! I sometimes go to formal dinner parties and my boyfriend says I don't look nice. But I don't want to look middle-aged!   Sindy L.

A Buy a "suit carrier"—that's a special bag for suits. You can take it on the plane. Put some comfortable loose clothes in the bag (for example, cotton pants and a light wool sweater). At the airport, go to the men's room, take off your suit and change into the loose clothing. When you arrive you can change back into your suit.

B Casual clothes can look nice! Try black or white jeans, a nice white top and a pretty jacket, but not sneakers! Buy some fashionable shoes and a matching belt.

C My answer is simple—layers! You and your children can put on extra clothes when you are cold and take them off when you are hot. For example, you can wear a T-shirt, a cotton shirt or top, a light sweater, and a coat. Put sunglasses, scarves, and gloves in your bags.

Vocabulary | clothes

2a Look for words in the advice column with opposite meanings.

Ex: hot _cold_____

1. uncomfortable _____   3. put on _____
2. casual _____   4. tight _____

b Look for these words in the column and match them to their meaning.

1. cotton   a. when things go together
2. wool   b. one thing on top of another thing
3. matching   c. fabric made from a plant
4. layers   d. fabric made from animal hair

3 **Pair Work** Look at the picture and say the names of the clothes for letters A–P.

Grammar | adverbs: frequency

4 Look at the advice column on page 78. Complete the Active Grammar box with the frequency adverbs *never*, *sometimes*, and *usually*. Then write *before* or *after* to complete the rules (1–2).

5 **Pair Work** Take turns rephrasing the sentences with the correct adverb of frequency.

> **Ex:** We go to the movies <u>twice a week</u>.

> *We often go to the movies.*

1. We go to the movies <u>once a month</u>.
2. He <u>doesn't</u> drink coffee.
3. He drinks coffee <u>with every meal</u>.
4. I take the dog for a walk <u>six days a week</u>.
5. I see my parents <u>once a year</u>.

Active Grammar

Frequency	Adverbs
100%	*always*
↑	_____
↑	*often*
↑	_____
↑	*hardly ever*
0%	_____

1. Put adverbs of frequency _____ the verb *be*.
2. Put adverbs of frequency _____ other verbs.

See Reference page 86

Speaking and Writing

6 **Pair Work** Ask and answer questions. Use adverbs of frequency.
1. What do you usually wear to work / to school / on weekends / on vacations?
2. What are your favorite shopping malls / stores / designer brands?

7a **SPEAKING EXCHANGE** Ask your partner for advice.
Student A: Look at page 129. **Student B:** Look at page 132.

b Write a letter requesting advice. Then write an answer to your partner's letter.

Describe what you are doing now CAN DO ✔

GRAMMAR present continuous; adverbs of manner

Listening

1a ▶ 2.08 Listen. The hosts of a reality TV show are watching seven people who live in one house. Write the number of the screen next to the names below.

_____ Adam and Rosa _____ Cara _____ Erica _____ Gary _____ Greg _____ Jason

b Write the correct names. Then listen again to check.

1. _____ is cycling in the gym.
2. _____ are talking.
3. _____ is digging in the garden.
4. _____ is preparing dinner.
5. _____ is looking for something.
6. _____ is crying.

Grammar | present continuous

2a Look at Exercise 1b again. Complete the Active Grammar box with the correct *be* verb.

Active Grammar

➕	➖	❓
I'm cycling.	I'm not cycling.	_Am_ I cycling?
He/She/It'_____ digging.	He/She/It _____ digging.	_____ he/she/it digging?
You/We/They'_____ shouting.	You/We/They _aren't_ shouting.	_____ you/we/they shouting?

See Reference page 86

b Look at Exercise 1b. Write the *-ing* forms.

1. look ➔ _looking_
2. dig ➔ _____
3. talk ➔ _____
4. cycle ➔ _____
5. cry ➔ _____
6. prepare ➔ _____

3a **Pair Work** Take turns making sentences about the people in the house.

Ex: Greg/shout   *Greg is shouting.*

1. Greg/not prepare breakfast   *Greg isn't ...*
2. Cara/not sleep
3. Jason/dig up flowers
4. Erica/not jog
5. Erica/sing
6. Adam and Rosa/not write

b **Pair Work** Describe a screen, but don't name the person. Ask your partner to guess the name.

Grammar | adverbs of manner

4a Look at the <u>underlined</u> words in the Active Grammar box. Then circle the correct words to complete the rules.

b Complete the sentences with these adverbs.

> carefully   happily   quietly   well

1. I couldn't hear him because he spoke very _____.
2. To get a job as a rep, you need to speak English _____.
3. Maria's singing _____. Is she having a good day?
4. Write your essays _____—I don't want to see any mistakes.

> **Active Grammar**
>
> *She's cycling <u>fast</u>. They're talking <u>quietly</u>.*
>
> *He's looking very <u>carefully</u>.*
>
> 1. Adverbs of manner give information about <u>the person doing the activity</u>/<u>the activity</u>.
> 2. They go <u>before</u>/<u>after</u> the verb.

See Reference page 86

Pronunciation | sentence rhythm

5a ▶2.09 Listen to the sentences. <u>Underline</u> the strong syllables. Then listen again and repeat.

Ex: She's <u>cy</u>cling <u>fast</u>.

1. They're talking quietly.
2. He's looking very carefully.
3. You're speaking loudly.
4. We're living there happily.

b **Group Work** Play a mime game. One student chooses a verb and an adverb to mime from the boxes below. The other students guess the activity.

> *Are you digging?*   *Yes, I am.*   *You're digging fast.*   *You're right.*

eat	teach	laugh	cycle	dance
dig	drink	walk	sleep	use a computer
run	swim	write	cook	play the guitar

badly	well	carefully	comfortably
fast	slowly	loudly	uncomfortably
happily	sadly	carelessly	

Speaking

6 **SPEAKING EXCHANGE** Ask and answer questions about the people in the pictures with a partner. Write the missing names.

Student A: Look at the picture on page 129.   **Student B:** Look at the picture on page 132.

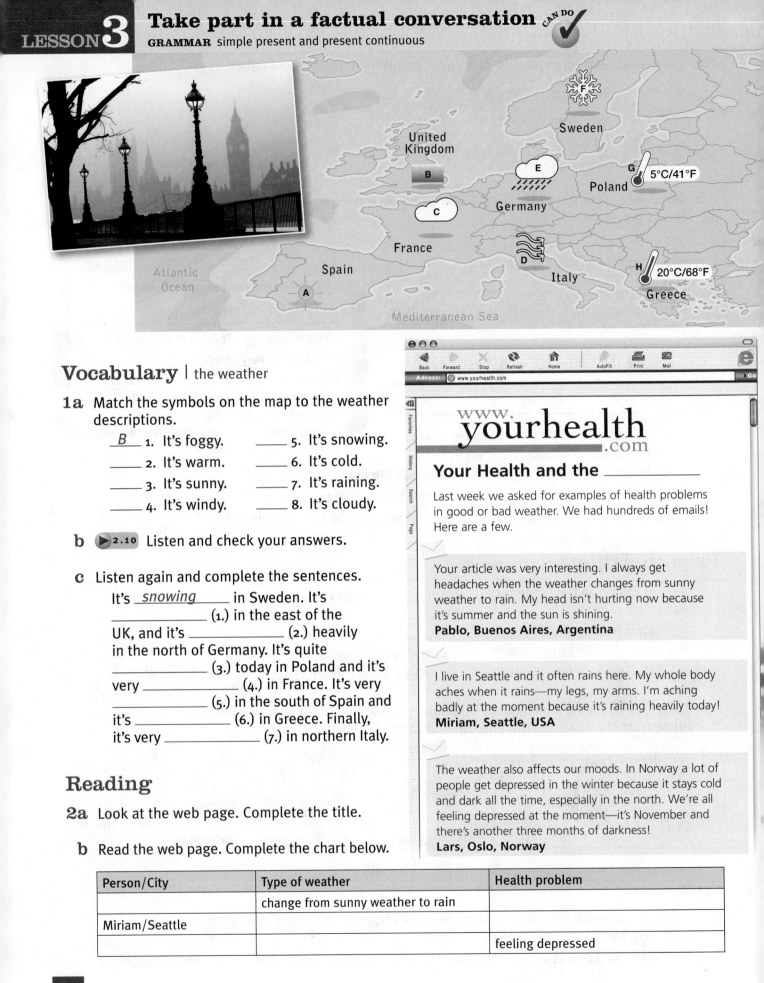

Vocabulary | the weather

1a Match the symbols on the map to the weather descriptions.

___B___ 1. It's foggy.   _____ 5. It's snowing.

_____ 2. It's warm.   _____ 6. It's cold.

_____ 3. It's sunny.   _____ 7. It's raining.

_____ 4. It's windy.   _____ 8. It's cloudy.

b ▶2.10 Listen and check your answers.

c Listen again and complete the sentences.
It's _snowing_____ in Sweden. It's _____ (1.) in the east of the UK, and it's _____ (2.) heavily in the north of Germany. It's quite _____ (3.) today in Poland and it's very _____ (4.) in France. It's very _____ (5.) in the south of Spain and it's _____ (6.) in Greece. Finally, it's very _____ (7.) in northern Italy.

Reading

2a Look at the web page. Complete the title.

b Read the web page. Complete the chart below.

---

www.yourhealth.com

Your Health and the _____

Last week we asked for examples of health problems in good or bad weather. We had hundreds of emails! Here are a few.

Your article was very interesting. I always get headaches when the weather changes from sunny weather to rain. My head isn't hurting now because it's summer and the sun is shining.
Pablo, Buenos Aires, Argentina

I live in Seattle and it often rains here. My whole body aches when it rains—my legs, my arms. I'm aching badly at the moment because it's raining heavily today!
Miriam, Seattle, USA

The weather also affects our moods. In Norway a lot of people get depressed in the winter because it stays cold and dark all the time, especially in the north. We're all feeling depressed at the moment—it's November and there's another three months of darkness!
Lars, Oslo, Norway

Person/City	Type of weather	Health problem
	change from sunny weather to rain	
Miriam/Seattle		
		feeling depressed

3 Match the words to their meanings.

_____ 1. ache   a. change, make different

_____ 2. heavily   b. sad and unhappy

_____ 3. affect   c. a lot

_____ 4. mood   d. hurt/feel bad

_____ 5. depressed   e. our feelings at one time

Speaking

4a ▶ **2.11** Listen to two people talking about the weather. Then read the How To box.

b **Pair Work** Have a conversation about the weather.

> Which season do you like best?

> Does the weather affect your health?

> Do you have allergies?

How To:	
Take part in a conversation	
Giving your opinion	*I think that it's the temperature.*
Agreeing	*Yes, I think so.*
Disagreeing	*I don't think so.*

Grammar | simple present and present continuous

5a Look at the web page again on page 82. <u>Underline</u> the verbs in the present continuous and circle the verbs in the simple present.

b Complete the rules in the Active Grammar box with *present continuous* or *simple present*.

Active Grammar

1. Use the _____ for actions happening now.
2. Use the _____ for actions that happen often, every year, etc.

See Reference page 86

6a **Pair Work** Look at the pictures. Take turns saying what the people usually do and what they are doing today.

    Ex: Peter—drive/sunbathe

> Peter usually drives a bus. Today he's sunbathing.

    1. Laura—walk to work/drive her new car

    2. Sally—clean the house/play soccer

    3. Anna—wear jeans/wear a dress

b **Pair Work** Ask and answer questions about the activities in the pictures.

> Is Laura walking to work today?

> No, she isn't. She's driving her new car.

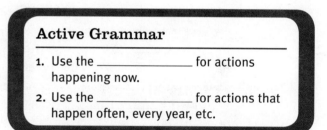

Review

1   Circle the best word or phrase.

> **Ex.** I am in shape because I *hardly ever*/*often* play sports.

1. Russians wear heavy coats in the winter because it is *never*/*usually* cold.
2. I don't like formal clothes. I *sometimes*/*hardly ever* wear a suit and tie.
3. Vegetarians *sometimes*/*never* eat meat.
4. Swiss watches *sometimes*/*hardly ever* cost a lot of money.

2a   Write the *-ing* form of these verbs.

> **Ex:** come ___*coming*___

1. dig _____
2. make _____
3. plan _____
4. read _____
5. carry _____
6. study _____
7. use _____
8. wait _____
9. write _____

b   Sandra is writing a letter to her friend. Fill in the blanks with some of the verbs from Exercise 2a in the present continuous.

> Dear Geena,
>
> Thanks for your letter. I _'m sitting_____ in Luigi's café at the moment – do you remember it?
> We had a really good meal here in March. I _____ (1.) this letter from here because
> I _____ (2.) for Jacob. He's in class at the moment; he _____ (3.) art.
> He _____ (4.) a computer in his classes and he really enjoys it — he _____ (5.)
> some amazing pictures on the computer. There's a travel guide to Canada on the table – do you
> know why? I _____ (6.) it because Jacob and I _____ (7.) a visit to Canada!

3a   Match the adverbs with their opposites.

_c_ 1. badly	a. quietly
____ 2. happily	b. uncomfortably
____ 3. loudly	c. well
____ 4. comfortably	d. unhappily

b   Complete the sentences with an adverb from Exercise 3a.

1. Julie watched Philip ___*unhappily*___.
2. He's shouting _____.
3. They're sitting _____.
4. "Shh! Please talk _____!"

4   Complete the sentences with the kind of clothes you usually wear. Share your sentences with a partner.

1. I wear _____ when it's snowing.
2. I wear _____ when it's raining.
3. I wear _____ for walks in the park.
4. I wear _____ when I go to work.

Communication | make a complaint in a store

5 Match the phrases to the pictures.

	Picture
1. it doesn't work	____
2. it doesn't fit	*A*
3. a receipt	____
4. a refund	____
5. an exchange	____

6 ▶ 2.12 Listen to dialogs 1 and 2 and match them to pictures A–E. Write 1 or 2 in the box next to each picture.

7a **Pair Work** Practice the dialogs from the Audioscript on page 141.

b Read the How To box.

How To:	
Make a complaint	
Ask for help	*Excuse me. Can you help me?*
Explain the situation	*I bought this jacket yesterday.*
Explain the problem	*It doesn't fit/work.*
Ask for an exchange/refund	*Can I exchange it?* *I'd like a refund.*

8 **SPEAKING EXCHANGE** Roleplay returning an item with a partner.

Student A: Look at the information below.
Student B: Turn to page 129.

Roleplay 1

You bought an Ace Technology C100 computer at Computer Central yesterday. You paid $1,250. It doesn't work because the screen is broken. You want to exchange it for another one.

Roleplay 2

You are a store clerk. Your store doesn't give refunds, but you can exchange things.

Unit 8 Reference

Adverbs of frequency

Use adverbs of frequency with the simple present to describe how regularly or how often something happens.

0%	→	→	→	→	100%
never	hardly ever	sometimes	often	usually	always

Put adverbs of frequency after the verb *be* but before other main verbs.

> The train **is usually** on time.
>
> The train **usually arrives** on time.

Present continuous

Make the present continuous with a present form of the verb *be* and the *-ing* form of the main verb.

⊕	I	'm	staying at home today.
	He / She / It	's	
	We / You / They	're	
⊖	I	'm not	staying at home today.
	He / She / It	isn't	
	We / You / They	aren't	
❓	Am	I	staying at home today?
	Is	he/she/it	
	Are	we/you/they	

Yes,	I am.	No,	I'm not.
	he/she/it is.		he/she/it isn't.
	we/you/they are.		we/you/they aren't.

Make this form by adding *-ing* to the base form of the verb, but note:

- with verbs that end in *-e*, remove *-e* and add *-ing*

  > cycle → cyc**ling**

- with verbs of one syllable that end in one short vowel + consonant, repeat the consonant and add *-ing*

  > dig → dig**ging**

Simple present and present continuous

Use the simple present to talk about routines—what is done every day/year—and to talk about facts.

> We always **have** pizza on Friday evenings.

Use the present continuous to talk about actions happening now, at the moment of speaking.

> We**'re having** our pizza now, so we can't talk to you at the moment.

Use phrases like *at the moment* and *(right)* now with the present continuous.

Use adverbs and expressions of frequency with the simple present.

Adverbs of manner

Use adverbs of manner with a verb. They describe the way that we do the action of the verb.

> She's running. → She's running **slowly**.

Adverbs of manner are usually formed from adjectives. Add *-ly* to most adjectives.

> quick → quick**ly**, loud → loud**ly**

When the adjective ends in *-y*, change *-y* to *-i* and add *-ly*.

> happy → happ**ily**, healthy → health**ily**

Some common adverbs are irregular.

> good → well, fast → fast

Adverbs of manner usually come after the verb, and often after any other words linked to the verb.

> I drank it quickly.

Unit Vocabulary

Clothes

hat	shirt	jeans	jacket	shorts
top	coat	scarf	shoes	sneakers
tie	suit	dress	T-shirt	sweater
belt	skirt	pants	gloves	boots

Clothes adjectives

tight	casual	heavy	comfortable
light	loose	formal	fashionable
thick	warm	informal	matching

The weather

It's sunny.	It's hot.	It's warm.
It's cold.	It's windy.	It's foggy.
It's snowing.	It's cloudy.	It's raining.

UNIT 9
Entertainment

A

B

C

D

Warm Up

1a Unscramble the words. Match the art forms to the photos.

_____ 1. s c i u m _____   _____ 3. r e t h e a t _____

_____ 2. e v o m i _____   _____ 4. a n i g n i p t _____

b Pair Work Look at the words in the box. Name an example of each.

| ballet | rock music | comedy | dance | novel | sculpture | contemporary art |
| opera | literature | cartoon | play | poetry | painting | classical music |

2   Group Work Discuss. What or who is one of your favorite:

• movies?   • books?   • operas or ballets?   • plays?   • groups or singers?

Reading

1a **Pair Work** Discuss.

1. What's in the news today?   2. How do you usually get the news?

b Label the photos in the article below with the names of the news sources from the box.

> Newspapers   Radio   TV   The Internet   Apps

Vocabulary | news media

2 Read the article and check (✓) the correct adjectives in the chart.

	Fast	Easy	Detailed	Cheap	New	Exciting	Convenient
Newspapers							
Radio							
TV							
The Internet							
Apps							

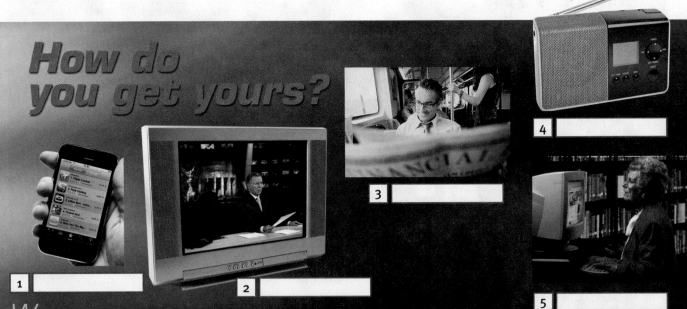

How do you get yours?

4 _____

3 _____

1 _____   2 _____

5 _____

We all like to know what's in the news—world news, local news, sports news—and today there are many different ways of finding out about recent events. How do people choose, and what do they like about the different methods?

Newspapers—still the favorite. Millions of people read newspapers because they're cheap, detailed, and you can read them at home, at work, or on the train.

Radio—people listen to the radio because it's easy. You can listen in the car, when you're working, or in bed, but some people think the radio is old-fashioned.

TV—almost everyone watches TV, and a lot of people get the news from it. It's interesting and exciting because it's visual. There are a lot of different kinds of news shows to suit all types of people.

The Internet—many people now use the Internet. It's detailed and very fast; news stories appear when they happen.

Apps—this way of getting news is popular because it's fast. The news arrives on your cell phone, so you get it anywhere, anytime.

Grammar | comparatives

3a ▶2.13 Listen and complete the sentences with the correct news sources.

1. _____ is <u>cheaper than</u> newspapers.
2. _____ are <u>faster than</u> TV.
3. _____ is <u>more detailed than</u> TV.
4. _____ is <u>more exciting than</u> newspapers.
5. _____ is <u>easier than</u> reading newspapers.
6. _____ is <u>better than</u> the radio.

b Complete the list of comparatives in the Active Grammar box with the <u>underlined</u> words in Exercise 3a. Then complete the rules (1–4).

c **Pair Work** Complete the sentences with the comparative form of the adjectives and another news source.

Ex: TV news is . . . (exciting)

> TV news is more exciting than newspapers.

1. Apps are . . . (immediate)
2. Newspapers are . . . (detailed)
3. The radio is . . . (good)

Active Grammar

Adjective	Comparative
fast	*faster than*
cheap	
easy	
detailed	
exciting	
good	
bad	*worse than*

1. Add *-er* to adjectives with one syllable only: _____*faster*_____
2. With adjectives that end in *-y*, change *-y* to *-i* and add *-er*: _____
3. With longer adjectives, use *more* before the adjective: _____
4. Some adjectives have irregular comparatives: _____

See Reference page 96

Pronunciation | /ɚ/ sound

4 ▶2.14 Listen to these phrases and <u>underline</u> the syllables with /ɚ/. Listen again and repeat.

Ex: eas<u>ie</u>r than   1. faster than   2. colder than   3. healthier than

Writing and Speaking

5a Complete the chart with your opinions.

	I like . . .	better than . . .
TV shows	*South Park*	*The Simpsons*
Newspapers		
Movie stars		
Books		
Types of food		
Holidays		

b Write sentences comparing the things in the chart. Give reasons.

> I like <u>South Park</u> better than <u>The Simpsons</u> because it's funnier.

6 **Pair Work** Compare your opinions with a partner.

Write a short film review CAN DO ✓

GRAMMAR superlatives

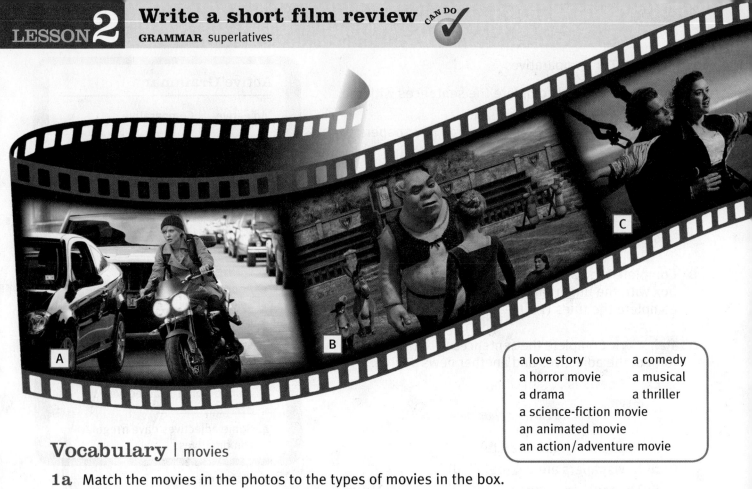

A

B

C

a love story	a comedy
a horror movie	a musical
a drama	a thriller

a science-fiction movie
an animated movie
an action/adventure movie

Vocabulary | movies

1a Match the movies in the photos to the types of movies in the box.

A = _____   C = _____

B = _____   D = _____

b **Pair Work** Name one movie from each type.

> Star Wars *is a science-fiction movie.*

Listening

2 ▶ **2.15** Listen to an interview and match the movies with the opinions.

_____ *Alice in Wonderland*   _____ *The Dark Knight*   _____ *Pirates of the Caribbean*   _____ *Shrek*

1. best animated movie   3. strangest   5. most interesting   7. most unusual

2. most exciting   4. funniest   6. scariest   8. most violent

Grammar | superlatives

3 Complete the Active Grammar box with the superlative adjectives from Exercise 2.

Active Grammar

To make the superlative, add *-est* to one or two syllable adjectives and put *the most* before longer adjectives.	Adjective	Superlative		Adjective	Superlative
	big	_the biggest_		interesting	_____
	exciting	_____		funny	_____
	strange	_____		violent	_____

See Reference page 96

D

Reading and Speaking

4a Read the movie quiz. Complete the questions with the adjectives in the superlative form.

b **SPEAKING EXCHANGE** Then complete the quiz in groups of three. Each student has three answers. Discuss the questions and match the answers to the correct question.

   Student A: Your answers are below.

   Student B: Turn to page 129.

   Student C: Turn to page 132.

   See page 129 for answers.

5 **Pair Work** Discuss.

   1. How many movies in the quiz have you heard of?

   2. What do you think is:
      • the most exciting action movie?
      • the most romantic love story?
      • the scariest horror movie?
      • the most boring movie?
      • the funniest comedy?
      • the best movie ever?

   3. Who is the best movie actor at the moment?

Movie Quiz
What do you know about movies?

1 What is _the most expensive_ movie ever made? (expensive)

2 What was _____ movie with sound? (early)

3 Which movie is the _____? (long)

4 What is _____ cartoon? (successful)

5 Who is _____ movie star? (rich)

6 Who is _____ Oscar winner? (young)

7 What is _____ love story? (romantic)

8 What is _____ horror movie? (scary)

9 Who is _____ villain in a movie? (bad)

Questions 1–6 are movie facts.
Questions 7–9 show the critics' choices.

Writing

6a Read the movie review.

b Number the information in the order it appears.

   _____ 1. the stars
   _____ 2. the writer's choice of film
   _____ 3. the story of the film
   _____ 4. the film's location
   _____ 5. a recommendation
   _____ 6. the type of film
   _____ 7. what the writer thinks is good about the film

c **Pair Work** Write a short movie review.

Movie Review

In my opinion, the best film of the last ten years was <u>The Dark Knight</u>, from 2008. It's a superhero thriller and it stars Heath Ledger and Christian Bale. The film is set in Gotham City, and it's about a battle between Batman and the Joker. It's very exciting and the acting is excellent. Go see it!

Student A

Psycho   Tatum O'Neal   *Shrek 2*

A

B

A Contemporary Artist

For many people, contemporary art is a mystery and difficult to understand: abstract paintings, sharks in glass boxes, and enormous animals. What do these works mean? Are they really art?

One contemporary artist is different. Most people understand and enjoy his work. He is the Bulgarian American artist Christo. He wraps buildings and geographical features in fabric. One of his most famous works is "The Gates" in Central Park. He put up more than 7,000 gates covered with orange fabric for 16 days in 2005.

We see everyday things in a new way in his work. And perhaps that is the greatest purpose of contemporary art.

Reading

1 **Pair Work** Look at the artworks and discuss. What do you see?

2a Read the article quickly. Match it to one of the pictures. _____

b **Pair Work** Read the article again. Then ask and answer the questions.

  1. Who is Christo?
  2. What is one of Christo's most famous works?
  3. What is the main purpose of contemporary art?

c **Pair Work** Find some words in the article that you don't understand. Use a dictionary to find the meanings and explain them to your partner.

Listening

3a ▶2.16 Listen to Jessie and Frank. Match the artists to the artworks in the photos.

  _D_ Christo _____ Damien Hirst _____ Fernando Botero

  _____ Roy Lichtenstein _____ Vincent Van Gogh

b Listen again. Match the types of art to some of the pictures. Circle the art that Jessie likes and <u>underline</u> the art that Frank likes.

  _____ 1. sculpture _____ 3. contemporary art
  _____ 2. impressionist painting _____ 4. pop art

4a Read the How To box.

b **Pair Work** Discuss which of the artworks you like better.

> Which do you like better, the Hirst or the Botero?

How To:	
Talk about preferences	
Express preferences	*I like traditional art better than contemporary art.*
Ask about preferences	*Which do you like better, the Van Gogh or the Lichtenstein?*

> I think I like the Hirst better. It's more interesting. How about you?

Grammar | *like* + noun/gerund

5a Circle the correct word to complete the examples in the Active Grammar box. Then circle the letters to complete the rule.

b **Group Work** Talk to your group and find out which of these things students like better:

1. dogs or cats
2. looking at art or going to concerts
3. watching videos or going to the movies
4. cold weather or hot weather
5. going to restaurants or eating at home
6. contemporary art or traditional art

Active Grammar

I like impressionist paintings better <u>than</u>/<u>to</u> sharks.

I like <u>sightsee</u>/<u>sightseeing</u> better than <u>look</u>/<u>looking</u> at art.

After *like* we can use:
a. a noun.
b. the base of a verb (*look*).
c. the *-ing* form (*looking*).

See Reference page 96

Grammar | *will*: spontaneous decisions/offers

6a ▶ 2.17 Jessie and Frank are in New York. Listen and check (✓) two places they plan to visit.
- [ ] Times Square
- [ ] Statue of Liberty
- [ ] Empire State Building
- [ ] Lincoln Center

b Listen again. Complete the statements in the Active Grammar box. Then circle the correct choice to complete the rule.

c **Pair Work** Look at the pictures and make offers to help. Use words and phrases from the box.

open	phone	find	look after
call	answer	carry	ambulance
door	mother	baby	bag

> *I'll open the door.*

Active Grammar

Jenny: *I'll get the _____.*

Jenny: *I'll look at the _____.*

Frank: *We'll go there after _____.*

Use *will* for decisions and offers that you make <u>before</u>/<u>at the time of</u> speaking.

In conversation and informal writing, use the contracted form *'ll*.

See Reference page 96

Review

1   Complete the paragraph with the comparative form of
the adjectives in parentheses.

Alan and Russell are brothers, but they look
different. Alan is _younger_____ (young) than
Russell. He is also _____ (1. tall) and
_____ (2. handsome) than his brother.
Alan is in _____ (3. good) shape than
Russell. Russell is _____ (4. heavy) than
Alan, but he is also _____ (5. happy)
than his brother. Alan has _____ (6. dark)
skin than Russell, and Russell has _____ (7. short) hair than his brother.

2   Complete the chart with the comparative and superlative forms
of the adjectives.

Adjective	Comparative	Superlative
1. bad	_worse_	_worst_
2. big		
3. beautiful		
4. crazy		
5. dry		
6. fit		
7. good		
8. informal		
9. noisy		
10. interesting		

3   Make sentences with superlatives.

Ex: small / country / Vatican City   _Vatican City is the smallest country._

1. big / structure in the world /
   the Great Wall of China   _____

2. high / mountain in Africa / Kilimanjaro   _____

3. large / museum in the world /
   the Hermitage Museum   _____

4. rich / country / Luxembourg   _____

5. famous / Mexican artist / Diego Rivera   _____

6. scary / movie / *Psycho*   _____

7. long / river in the world / the Nile   _____

4   Find the mistakes in each sentence and fix or write the correction.

Ex: Lucinda doesn't like tennis; she likes ~~play~~ golf. _playing_____

1. I like the radio, but my children like to watching television. _____

2. We reading books like. _____

3. Isabel likes romantic movies than science-fiction ones. _____

4. Some people are liking living in the country. _____

5. The bus is very slow, so I like drive my car to work. _____

Communication | discuss and plan activities

5a **Pair Work** What do you usually do on Saturdays? Make a list with a partner.

b ▶2.18 Listen to these friends and check (✓) the things they decide to do on Saturday.
☐ go swimming ☐ watch a movie ☐ have lunch ☐ go shopping

c Listen again. Then read the How To box.

How To:	
Discuss and plan activities	
Make suggestions	*How about a movie?* *Why don't we go to the pool?* *Let's go to the mall in the morning.*
Express preferences	*I don't like watching movies during the day.* *I like shopping better than swimming.*
Make comparisons	*The stores are more expensive there.*
Decide what to do	*OK. We'll meet at eleven outside the main entrance.*

6a Look at this list of things to do with a friend in the evening. Which activity do you prefer? Rank them in order 1–10 (1 is your favorite).

_____ see a play   _____ have dinner at a nice restaurant

_____ go to a nightclub   _____ go shopping at the mall

_____ see a movie   _____ go to a classical concert

_____ go bowling   _____ go to a rock concert

_____ see an opera   _____ go to a soccer game

b Circle the activities that you see in the photos.

c **Pair Work** Compare the order of your lists. Ask about your partner's list and explain your preferences.

> *My number 1 is "go to a classical concert" because I like classical music more than any other kind of music.*

7a **Group Work** Organize an evening out.
1. Ask about your classmates' preferences and find something you all like to do.
2. Talk about the things you can do in your area and make suggestions for tomorrow evening.
3. Agree on a plan for the evening and arrange a time and a place to meet.

b Invite another friend to join you. Write a short text message to him or her with information about your group's arrangement.

> Plans for tomorrow:
> Meet at . . .

Unit 9 Reference

Comparatives

Use comparative adjectives to compare two or more things.

This house is bigger than my old house.

Regular one-syllable adjectives

old → older, cheap → cheaper, thick → thicker

Longer adjectives

*interesting → **more** interesting*
*comfortable → **more** comfortable*

Two-syllable adjectives that end in -y

scary → scarier

Irregular adjectives

good → better, bad → worse

Use *than* to introduce the second noun in a comparative sentence.

*This book is **more interesting than** his first book.*

Superlatives

Use superlative adjectives to compare one thing with all the others in a group.

*The blue shoes are **the most expensive** in the store.*

Regular one-syllable adjectives

old → oldest, cheap → cheapest, thick → thickest

Longer adjectives

*interesting → **most** interesting*
*comfortable → **most** comfortable*

Two-syllable adjectives that end in -y

scary → scariest

Irregular adjectives

good → best, bad → worst

English speakers usually use *the* before a superlative.

*This is **the** most interesting book in the library.*

Spelling rules

- add *-r/-st* to adjectives that end in *-e*
  nice → nicer/nicest, large → larger/largest
- with adjectives that end in consonant + *-y*, change *-y* to *-i* and add *-er/-est*
  busy → busier/busiest, heavy → heavier/heaviest
- with adjectives that end in a short vowel + consonant, double the consonant and add *-er/-est*
  thin → thinner/thinnest, big → bigger/biggest

like + noun/gerund

Use *like* with a noun or the *-ing* form of another verb.

*I **like** tea.   I **like drinking** tea.*

will: spontaneous decisions/offers

Use *will* + the base form of a verb to do something or make an offer to do something at the same time as speaking. The action usually happens in the immediate or near future.

A: *John. There's somebody knocking on our door.*
B: *OK. **I'll answer it.***

In spoken English, use the contraction *'ll*, not *will*.

A: *Can somebody help me with these bags?*
B: *We'll do it.*

Unit Vocabulary

The arts

Fine arts:
painting
(contemporary/impressionist/traditional/pop art)
sculpture

Performance arts:
ballet
classical music/rock music
dance
movie
opera
play
theater

Movie genres:

a comedy	a drama	a horror movie
a musical	a thriller	a love story
a science-fiction movie		an animated movie
an action/adventure movie		

UNIT 10
Going places

Warm Up

1   Match the photos to the captions.

_____ 1. Businessmen traveling to a meeting by private jet.

_____ 2. Commuting by train from the suburbs into Taipei.

_____ 3. Rush hour traffic in Los Angeles.

_____ 4. Cycling to the office.

2   Match the words to the meanings.

1. commuting   a. full of people
2. suburbs   b. traveling to work every day
3. park   c. the busiest time of day
4. rush hour   d. cars moving on a road
5. crowded   e. leave a car somewhere
6. traffic   f. places around a city where people live

Listening

1a ▶ 2.19 Listen to an excerpt from a TV show.

    1. Where is the family going? _____

    2. What will they do there? _____

b Read this quote from the TV show:

    Derek: I've never been on a really long flight before, so it's my first time.

    Is the plane trip Derek's first long flight? _____

c Listen again. Will they do these things for the first time in Australia? Or will it be their second time? Write *1ˢᵗ* or *2ⁿᵈ* in the chart.

	Moira	Derek	Todd	Alicia
Long flight	2ⁿᵈ	1ˢᵗ		
Visit Australia				
Horseback riding				
Hiking				
Bungee jumping				

d **Group Work** Discuss. Which activity do you think is the most exciting?

Grammar | *be:* present perfect

2a **Pair Work** Read the quotes in the box from the TV show and answer the questions below.

> a. "I've never been on a really long flight before."
>
> b. "We went horseback riding when we were in Montana two years ago."

1. Which quote refers to a particular time in the past? When?
2. Which quote does not refer to a particular time in the past?
3. Which tense is used when not referring to a particular time in the past?

b Read the Audioscript on page 142 and complete the Active Grammar box.

> **Active Grammar**
>
> **+** subject + *'ve* (or *have*) + past participle
> *We've _____ to Mexico City.*
>
> **−** subject + *haven't* (or *have never*) + past participle
> *We _____ _____ bungee jumping.*
>
> **?** *Have* + subject (+ *ever*) + past participle
> *Have _____ ever _____ to Australia?*
> *Yes, I/we/you/they have.   No, I/we/you/they _____.*

See Reference page 106

3a Complete the questions and answers.

1. A: Have you _____ been to Taiwan?
   B: Yes, I _____.
2. A: _____ your mother ever been to the opera?
   B: No, she _____.
3. A: Have you ever _____ to Canada?
   B: Yes, we _____ last summer, and it was great!

b **Pair Work** Ask and answer questions with *ever* about the pictures on page 98.

Speaking

4 **SPEAKING EXCHANGE** Work in groups of three. Ask your partners questions.
Student A: Look at page 130.   Student B: Look at page 132.   Student C: Look at this page.

	Student C	
A: *Have you ever been to an IMAX theater?*	• an IMAX theater?	• a theme park?
B: *Yes, I have. I went to one last week.*	• a bullfight?	• a wedding?
A: *Did you like it?*	• a circus?	• a rock concert?

Reading

1a Read the brochure below. What can you do at Seagaia? _____

b Match the adjectives to their meanings.

1. luxurious
2. artificial
3. first-class
4. exclusive

a. the best of its type
b. not real
c. very comfortable and beautiful
d. expensive; for a few people

2a Read the brochure again. Write questions for the following answers.

1. a luxurious resort *What is Seagaia?* _____
2. in Japan _____
3. an indoor beach and sea _____
4. in hotels, cottages, or apartments _____
5. the zoo, theme park, and gardens _____

b **Pair Work** Discuss. What do you think of Seagaia? Does this type of vacation interest you? Why or why not?

Have you ever sunbathed on a rainy day? No?
Well, at Phoenix Seagaia, you can!

Seagaia is a luxurious resort on Japan's Pacific coast. The Ocean Dome is the largest indoor artificial beach and sea. The water is warm, clean, and safe, and the roof of the Dome opens when it's sunny but closes in bad weather.

But Seagaia isn't only the Ocean Dome.

There's a lot more here:
- stay in a first-class hotel, a comfortable cottage, or a traditional Japanese apartment
- play golf on our world-class courses
- surf and sail in the Pacific Ocean
- improve your tennis and golf at our exclusive clubs
- visit the wonderful zoo, theme park, and gardens

For the vacation of a lifetime, choose Phoenix Seagaia!

Grammar | present perfect

3a **Pair Work** Read the postcard. Who is it from? Where was she at the time she wrote it?

b Underline the present perfect verbs in the postcard and write them in the chart below.

Regular verb	Irregular verb
have arrived	has been

> Dear Karen,
> Well, we've arrived at Seagaia, and it's amazing! We're staying in a nice Japanese apartment.
> The weather has been wonderful, so I've spent hours at the Ocean Dome — the water's great. I've seen the golf courses, but I haven't played any golf.
> Patrick has had a great time in the sea. He has been surfing, sailing, and swimming. Melanie loves animals, so she's visited the zoo. She's also taken a surfing lesson.
> Well, it's time for dinner. See you soon.
> Love, Lara

c Circle the correct choice to complete the rule in the Active Grammar box.

> **Active Grammar**
>
> Lara uses the present perfect to describe her vacation activities because she is still on vacation / her vacation has ended .

See Reference page 106

4 Complete the text with the present perfect of the verbs in parentheses.

> We _have arrived_____ (arrive) at our hotel. It has a fantastic swimming pool, and Leon and I _____ (1. go) swimming. Zosia and Basia _____ (2. not spend) any time in the sea because they noticed the tennis court — they _____ (3. play) three games of tennis so far! I _____ (4. also spend) an hour in the spa — so relaxing. Leon _____ (5. visit) the town and he _____ (6. see) some interesting things, but he _____ (7. not take) any photos — he forgot his camera.

Pronunciation | long and short vowels

5a ▶2.20 Listen to these long and short vowels. Then repeat the words.

Long vowels	Short vowels
/eɪ/ hate /i/ seen /əʊ/ gold	/æ/ had /ɪ/ hit /ɒ/ got

b ▶2.21 Listen. Circle the word you hear.

1. have   hate   3. show   shop   5. at   ate
2. feet   fit   4. meet   mit   6. sleep   slip

Speaking and Writing

6a **Pair Work** Imagine you are on vacation. Discuss the questions and make notes on your own answers.

1. Where are you?
2. Where are you staying?
3. What has the weather been like?
4. What have you done?

b Write a postcard. Use your notes from Exercise 6a.

City Profiles

This week we look at commuters around the world . . .

Dan Rodgers works for San Francisco's BART, the Bay Area Rapid Transit rail system that connects the outlying suburbs and towns with the city. But Dan doesn't catch a train to work. He rides a bicycle to work from his apartment in the city. Cycling is popular in San Francisco because distances are not that great. Cycling is also very good exercise. Dan likes cycling to work, but sometimes the steep hills tire him out.

Fatima da Costa lives in Patriarca, a suburb in the east of São Paulo, Brazil. She works in the center of the city, near Praça Republica. Every day Fatima takes the subway to work in the morning and back home in the evening. She thinks traveling on the São Paulo subway system—the Metro—is quick and convenient. But the trains are very crowded during rush hour, and she often can't find a seat.

American English	British English
subway	underground

Reading

1 Read the article and complete the chart for Fatima and Dan.

Name	Picture	City	Transportation	Advantages	Disadvantages
Dan					steep hills
Fatima				quick,	

Grammar | gerund as subject

2 Find and <u>underline</u> two examples of the *-ing* form in the article. Then circle the correct words to complete the sentences in the Active Grammar box.

3 **Pair Work** Take turns making sentences from the cues.

Ex: park/impossible/downtown (*Parking is impossible downtown.*)

1. walk/to work/good exercise
2. cycle/in the city/dangerous
3. wait/for a bus/boring
4. ride/the train/relaxing
5. take/taxis/expensive
6. live/in a big city/exciting

> ### Active Grammar
> 1. Swimming <u>is</u> / are my favorite sport.
> 2. <u>Parking</u> / Park isn't easy in the city.

See Reference page 106

Speaking

4 **Group Work** Discuss.

1. Complete the questions with words from the box. Which form of transportation is:

- the safest?
- the most expensive?
- the cheapest?
- the most convenient?
- the fastest?
- the most comfortable?

2. Which form of commuting is best? Why?

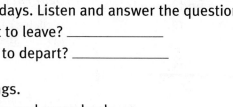

car	ferry	subway
taxi	bicycle	helicopter
bus	carpool	motorcycle
train	on foot	

Listening

5a ▶2.22 Mika is on vacation in Hawaii. She and her three friends have decided to visit Maui for a few days. Listen and answer the questions.

1. What day does Mika want to leave? _____
2. What time would she like to depart? _____

b Match the words to the meanings.

1. destination — a. go and come back
2. one-way — b. more comfortable but expensive seats
3. round-trip — c. the place you want to go to
4. economy class — d. when you leave
5. business class — e. no stops
6. departure — f. go to your destination only
7. direct — g. the cheapest seats

c **Pair Work** Look at the Audioscript on page 142. Practice the dialog with a partner. Then read the How To box.

How To:	
Book a ticket	
Ask for information	*Do you sell discount air tickets to Maui?*
Give details	*We'd like to leave this Friday.* *We'd like to come back on Monday.*
Ask for more information	*Are there any stops?* *What time does the flight leave?*
Ask for tickets	*I'd like four tickets, please.*
Ask about prices	*What's the total?*

6 **SPEAKING EXCHANGE** Roleplay asking about flights.

Student A: You are a travel agent. Turn to page 130.

Student B: You want to book a flight. Look at the information to the right, and then telephone the travel agent. Which airline will you choose?

You want to fly from New York's JFK airport to Miami with a friend. You want to leave next Wednesday and return a week later. You don't want to spend more than $1,000 total. Call the travel agent; get information about flights, dates, and prices; and then book your tickets.

Review

1 Put the words in the correct order to make sentences.

Ex: been / to / China / Have / ever / you / ? _____*Have you ever been to China?*_____

1. never / a long / I've / flight / been / on _____

2. cruise / you / been / Have / ever / on / a / ? _____

3. to / We've / New York and Boston / been _____

4. horseback riding / in / been / She's / Scotland _____

2 Max and Lorena are on vacation in India. Look at the list of things they have and haven't done and complete Max's postcard.

	Max	Lorena
see the Taj Mahal	✓	✓
visit the Bollywood studios	✗	✗
eat lots of Indian food	✗	✓
go swimming in the Indian Ocean	✓	✗
take an elephant ride	✓	✓
buy some spices	✗	✓
play golf with some friends	✓	✗
go on a boat trip	✓	✓

Dear Paul,

Well, we're in India — the vacation of a lifetime! _We've seen_ the Taj Mahal — it's amazing — but _we haven't visited_ the Bollywood studios. _____ (1.) lots of Indian food, of course — she loves Indian food — but I have only eaten in the hotel. _____ (2.) in the Indian Ocean. Lorena hasn't because she's worried about sharks! _____ (3.) an elephant ride. That was interesting, but not very comfortable. _____ (4.) some spices at the market and _____ (5.) with some friends. _____ (6.) on a boat trip. It was really relaxing.

See you soon.

Love, Max

3 Complete the sentences with a verb in the box. Then share your sentences with a partner.

fly	swim	take	commute
pay	drive	stay	

Ex: _*Flying*_ in business class is quite expensive.

1. _____ by credit card is very convenient.

2. _____ is a good way to get in shape.

3. _____ at resorts is fun.

4. _____ a fast car is very exciting.

5. _____ the train is relaxing.

6. _____ takes a long time in big cities.

4 Complete each sentence with a travel word.

1. It doesn't stop. It's a _____ flight.

2. Excuse me. Can I have a _____ ticket? I want to come back tomorrow.

3. I like flying in business _____ because the seats are more comfortable.

4. There are two stops before we arrive at our _____.

5. I may not come back, so I bought a _____ ticket.

6. You can _____ a ticket at a travel agency.

Communication | understand basic hotel information, reserve a hotel room

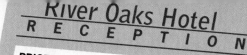

River Oaks Hotel
R E C E P T I O N

PRICES
Standard room (1 queen bed/2 double beds) $169
Deluxe room (1 king bed/2 double beds) $199
Suite (1 king bed, living room) $259
Breakfast Buffet $22 (6 A.M.–10 A.M.)

FACILITIES AND SERVICES
Restaurant 6 A.M.–9 P.M.
Lounge 3 P.M.–11:30 P.M.
Swimming pool 8 A.M.–10 P.M. (free to guests)
Gym/sauna 8 A.M.–10 P.M. (free to guests)
Spa 10 A.M.–7 P.M. (price list at reception)
Tennis/golf 10 A.M.–7 P.M. (price list at reception)

5 **Pair Work** Look at the hotel information. Take turns asking and answering the questions.

1. What kinds of rooms are available? What kinds of beds do they have?
2. What facilities and services are there? How much are spa treatments?

6a ▶2.23 Listen to someone reserving a room at this hotel. What kind of room does she reserve and for when? Does she want anything else?

b Read the How To box.

How To:	
Reserve a hotel room	
Ask to reserve a room	*I'd like to reserve a room, please.*
Say which type of room	*I'd like a standard room with two double beds.*
Ask about the services	*And do you have a spa?*

7 **Pair Work** Take turns reserving a hotel room.

Student A: Close your book. Then decide on the type of room you want, the dates, and anything else you want. Call Student B (the receptionist).

Student B: You are the receptionist. Use the hotel information and your imagination to answer Student A. Then change roles.

8a ▶2.24 Listen to the complaints and complete the chart.

b SPEAKING EXCHANGE Roleplay making a complaint.
Student A: Look at the information below.
Student B: Turn to page 130.

	The guest asked for . . .	What happened?
1.		
2.		

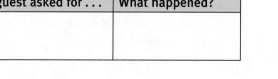

Reception. Can I help you?   *Yes, I'm afraid there's a problem. I reserved . . .*

Roleplay 1
You are the guest. You reserved a standard room with two double beds, but they have given you a room with one queen bed. Make a complaint.

Roleplay 2
You are the receptionist. Apologize and offer to ask the kitchen to send breakfast right away (*I'll ask . . .*).

Unit 10 Reference

Present perfect

Form the present perfect with *has/have* + the past participle (*been*).

	I/You/We/They	He/She/It
⊕	*'ve (have)* + past participle	*'s (has)* + past participle
⊖	*haven't (have not)* + past participle	*hasn't (has not)* + past participle
	OR *have* + *never* + past participle	OR *has* + *never* + past participle
?	*Have* + *I/we/you/they (+ ever)* + past participle	*Has* + *he/she/it (+ ever)* + past participle
	Yes, I/we/you/they have.	*Yes, he/she/it has.*
	No, I/we/you/they haven't.	*No, he/she/it hasn't.*

The past participle of most verbs is the same as the regular simple past form.

Base form	Simple past	Past participle
play	*played*	*played*
arrive	*arrived*	*arrived*

There are a lot of irregular past participles. Some of them are the same as the simple past form.

Base form	Simple past	Past participle
buy	*bought*	*bought*
have	*had*	*had*

Many of them are different from the simple past form.

Base form	Simple past	Past participle
see	*saw*	*seen*
take	*took*	*taken*

Note that the past participle *been* can be used for both *be* and *go*.

> *It's a nice day.* → *It's been a nice day.*
> *I go shopping on Saturdays.* → *I haven't been shopping this week.*

Use the present perfect to talk about actions in the past when:

- talking about any time up to now *Have you ever been to Japan?*
- not saying a definite time *We've met the president.*
- it is still possible to do/repeat an action (because the time is still continuing) *Keith has written four books.* (He can write another book because he is still alive.)

Use the present perfect with *ever/never* to talk about experiences at any time up to and including the present.

> *Have you **ever** been to Rome?   No, I've **never** been to Italy.*

Don't use the present perfect with a specific past time. Use the simple past form.

> *I **didn't have** a vacation last year.*
> *We **saw** her yesterday.*

Use the present perfect to talk about a past experience for the first time.

> *We've **been** to Florida . . .*

But when giving more information, use the simple past.

> *We **went** to Miami two years ago.*

gerund as subject

Use the *-ing* form of a verb as the subject of a sentence.

> ***Parking** is really difficult in Lima.*

Use singular verbs with *-ing* verb subjects.

> *Flying **is** expensive.*

Unit Vocabulary

Travel

commuting	departure
destination	rush hour traffic
one-way/round trip	

Flying:

direct flight	first class
economy class/business class	

Hotels

Rooms:

deluxe	double bed
suite	queen bed
king bed	standard

Facilities and Services:

spa	lounge
gym	exclusive
golf	restaurant
sauna	luxurious
tennis	artificial
swimming pool	

UNIT 11
Education

A

B

C

D

Warm Up

1a **Pair Work** Put the words and phrases from the box into the correct column in the chart.

math	chemistry	high school
history	geography	middle school
physics	pre-school	university/college
biology	psychology	elementary school
literature	kindergarten	PE/physical education

Educational institutions	School subjects

b **Pair Work** What classes do photos A–D show? Add these subjects to the chart.

LESSON 1 **Understand signs and rules**
GRAMMAR permission: *can/can't*,
obligation: *have to/don't have to*

Reading

1 **Group Work** Discuss.

1. Do you drive? Do you enjoy driving?
2. Do you always obey the rules of the road?
3. What happens when people break rules in your country?
   - fines • prison
   - points on their license

2a Read the article quickly. What is it about? _____

b Read the article again. Mark the statements true (*T*) or false (*F*).

_____ 1. You can't drive after you get a certain number of points on your license.

_____ 2. Offenders have to take a course at traffic school.

_____ 3. You have to pay to take traffic school courses.

_____ 4. Offenders at traffic school have to pass a driving test.

c **Pair Work** Discuss. Do you think traffic school is a good idea? Does this happen in your country?

Traffic School

Have you ever driven faster than the speed limit or driven through a red light? The answer is probably "yes." Every year thousands of drivers become "offenders"—they break traffic laws. But what are the punishments for this offense?

In most countries, drivers have to pay a fine, usually $100–$400. But in the United States, Australia, and some European countries, offenders also get points on their driver's license. After they get a certain number of points, they can't drive.

Life is difficult when you can't drive, so some states in the US have introduced a new way to give offenders a second chance—traffic school. Offenders have a choice: they can get points on their license or they can take a course at traffic school.

Traffic schools run "driver improvement courses." They cost about $80 and take eight hours. Drivers learn the reasons for traffic laws and they learn how to be better drivers. They don't have to take a driving test, but at the end of the course they have to pass a written exam.

Grammar | *can/can't, have to/don't have to*

3 Match the pictures to the explanations.

_____ 1. You **can pay** by credit card.

_____ 2. He **doesn't have to** have a driver's license.

_____ 3. You **can't smoke**.

_____ 4. You **have to wear** a seat belt.

_____ 5. You **don't have to pay**.

_____ 6. She **has to show** her passport.

See Reference page 116

| 4 | 5 | 6 | 7 ONLY | 8 | 9 | 10 |

4 Look at the road signs above. Write the rules with *can*, *can't*, or *have to*. Use the words and phrases in the box.

| turn right | stop | ~~yield~~ | get food | ~~go over 50 miles an hour~~ |
| turn left | park | get gas | make a U turn | watch for pedestrians |

Ex: 1. *You have to yield.*   **2.** *You can't go over 50 miles an hour.*

5 ▶2.25 Listen to information about driving in the United States and complete the form with *can*, *can't*, *have to*, or *don't have to*.

> ### DRIVING IN THE UNITED STATES
>
> **Visitors to the United States with a valid driving license usually:**
>
> ● _____ have an International Driver's License.
> ● _____ get an International Driver's License in their home country.
>
> **To rent a car, you usually:**
>
> ● _____ have a credit card. Debit cards require a deposit.
> ● _____ be 21 or over.
> ● _____ pay an extra fee if you are under 25.

Speaking

6 **Pair Work** Ask and answer the questions. In your country, what do you have to do to:

- get a passport?
- rent a car?
- get into college?
- get a credit card?
- open a bank account?
- get a cell phone account?

7a ▶2.26 Listen to Brian talking about the United States and take notes.

Ex: military service *don't have to do*

1. identity cards _____
2. driving _____
3. guns _____
4. nightclubs _____
5. smoking _____
6. doctors and hospitals _____

b **Group Work** Work in small groups. Compare the rules in the United States with your country's rules.

> *In my country, you have to do military service when you are 18.*

A   B   C

Reading

1 Group Work Discuss.

1. Which photos show students in: pre-school or kindergarten, elementary or middle school, high school, and college?

2. What do you call these educational institutions in your country?

2a Pair Work Read the article and answer the questions.

1. How many years do students have to attend school in the United States?

2. When do students start school?

3. How many years are students in elementary school?

4. What do you call a student in the 9th grade?

5. What degree do students get after four years of college? after six? after eight or nine?

b Pair Work Look at the chart. At what ages do students start elementary school, middle school, and high school in the United States?

Listening

3a ▶2.27 Listen to an interview with Nicole Gardener of New Zealand. Complete the chart for New Zealand. Listen again if necessary.

THE EDUCATIONAL SYSTEM IN THE UNITED STATES

The educational system in the United States varies because each state has a slightly different system. In all states, students have to go to school until they are at least 15 and, in some states, 18. Most students in the US go to school for 13 years (kindergarten through 12th grade), and many go on to college.

Most children go to kindergarten at the age of five, although many children start school earlier. Children can enroll in pre-school at the age of three or four.

Children usually begin the first grade, in elementary school, when they are six years old. In the sixth grade, students go to middle school (also called "junior high school"). Then in the ninth grade they enter high school. Students in high school are known as "freshmen" (9th grade), "sophomores" (10th grade), "juniors" (11th grade), and "seniors" (12th grade).

Some students end their education when they graduate from high school, but many go on to four-year colleges or universities in order to get a bachelor's degree. Some students continue in college another two years to get a master's degree, or four to five more years to get a doctorate. Students must pay for higher education. Community colleges and state universities are usually less expensive than private schools.

Age	United States	New Zealand	Your country
3	Pre-School		
4			
5	Kindergarten		
6	Elementary School		
7			
8			
9			
10			
11	Middle School		
12			
13			
14	High School		
15			
16			
17			
18	College		
19			
20			
21			

American English	British English
elementary school middle and high school	primary school secondary school

b Listen again and answer the questions.

1. How many years do students have to go to school (compulsory education)? _____

2. Why did Nicole go to a college of education? How long was she there? _____

3. How much do students pay for college? _____

Grammar | review of *wh-* questions

4 Match the words to complete the questions.

_____ 1. How long   a. years were you in elementary school?

_____ 2. When   b. did you go after high school?

_____ 3. How many   c. did you start school?

_____ 4. What   d. does a student have to pay?

_____ 5. Where   e. subjects did you take?

_____ 6. How much   f. do students spend in school?

See Reference page 116

Pronunciation | question intonation

5a ▶2.28 Listen. Does the voice go up (↗) or down (↘) at the end?

_____ 1. What did you do there?   _____ 3. Who did you see?

_____ 2. Was it interesting?   _____ 4. Did you like it?

b ▶2.29 Listen and repeat the questions in Exercise 5a.

Speaking

6 **Group Work** Write ten *wh-* questions to ask about a person's education. Ask and answer questions in small groups.

Writing

7a Complete the Your Country column in the chart on page 110.

b Using the chart and the article on page 110, write a short explanation of your country's educational system for an international students' magazine.

Reading

1a Pair Work Read the email quickly. What does Joanna plan to do? Where?

b Read again and mark the sentences true (*T*) or false (*F*).

_____ 1. Joanna will quit work.

_____ 2. She wants to study languages.

_____ 3. The Open University offers distance-learning classes.

_____ 4. Joanna can study from home.

c Match 1–3 to the <u>underlined</u> words in the email.

1. teacher _____

2. don't have the money to do something _____

3. learning from home, away from a school/college _____

○○○ ⬤

Hi Marisa,

I've got some interesting news — I'm going back to school! My job is a bit boring now, but I <u>can't afford</u> to leave work, so I've joined the Open University. I'm starting next month (January) and I'm working towards a degree in art history. As you know, I don't have a college degree, so I think it's a good idea. It's a <u>distance-learning</u> program, so I can study at home in my free time. You can have a personal <u>tutor</u> who helps you. I'll tell you all about it when I start.

By the way, we're going skiing next week, before my classes start, and Jim is going to Mexico again in March — he organized it all last week. Are you doing anything exciting in the next few weeks?

Love,
Joanna

Grammar | future with present continuous

2a Look at the sentences in the Active Grammar box and answer the question.

b <u>Underline</u> five examples of the present continuous for future in the email.

3a Look at the daily calendar of activities for four roommates. Write sentences in the present continuous.

> Kimiko is cooking dinner for her friends on Monday.

b Pair Work What plans do you have for these times? Discuss.

on Friday evening / on Saturday afternoon / on Sunday / the weekend after next

> *What are you doing on Friday evening?*

> *I'm going to a concert.*

Active Grammar

I'm starting next month . . .

Jim is going to Mexico again in March . . .

Are the sentences describing an action in the present or in the future? _____

See Reference page 116

Monday	Kimiko — cook dinner for friends, 7:30
Tuesday	Juan and Pilar — go to a movie, 8:45
Wednesday	Radek — start his new English class, 6:30
Thursday	Juan — meet his brother at the Italian restaurant, 8:00
Friday	everyone — go to a nightclub, 10:30
Saturday	Kimiko — take a flight to Tokyo, 11:50

Listening

4a ▶2.30 Listen to three people. Write 1–3 by the ads in the order the speakers talk about them.

☐

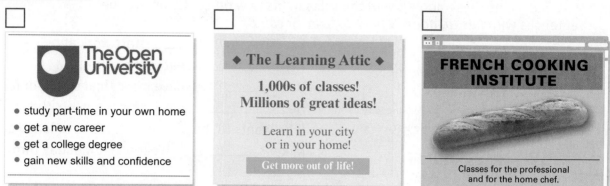

The Open University

- study part-time in your own home
- get a new career
- get a college degree
- gain new skills and confidence

☐

♦ **The Learning Attic** ♦

1,000s of classes!
Millions of great ideas!

Learn in your city
or in your home!

Get more out of life!

☐

FRENCH COOKING INSTITUTE

Classes for the professional
and for the home chef.

b Listen again and complete the chart.

	Open University	French Cooking Institute	The Learning Attic
Where do you study?		*in kitchens at the institute*	
How long is a class?			
How much does it cost?			
Examples of subjects	*art, biology, history*		

Vocabulary | education

5 Review the words in the box. Write three sentences about education. Use words from the box.

afford	online	classroom	college	adult education
career	institute	degree	instruction	distance-learning
cost	part-time	instructor	university	

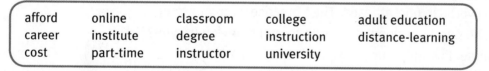

I'm interested in online
distance-learning classes.

Speaking

6 **Group Work** Discuss.

1. What kinds of adult education schools and classes are there in your country?
2. Have you taken any adult education courses?
3. What adult education courses would you like to take in the future?
4. What do you think about online distance-learning college programs?

Review

1   Mike has made these notes about the rules in his new office. Complete the sentences with *has to, doesn't have to, can,* or *can't.*

Office rules
— Hours are from 9 A.M. to 5:30 P.M.
— But OK to go home at 4 P.M. on Wednesdays.
— One hour for lunch (but anytime between 12 and 3).
— No eating or drinking in the office.
— Don't make personal phone calls.
— But personal email from my computer is OK.
— Don't use my cell phone in the office.
— Wear a suit and tie, but informal clothes OK on Fridays.

Ex: Mike ___*has to*___ start work at nine o'clock.

1. He _____ eat in the office.
2. He _____ have more than one hour for lunch.
3. He _____ leave after 4 P.M. on Wednesdays.
4. If he wants to, he _____ have lunch at two.
5. Mike _____ wear a suit Monday through Thursday.
6. He _____ make personal phone calls.
7. He _____ use his cell phone in the office.
8. He _____ wear a suit on Fridays.
9. He _____ send personal emails.

2   Complete the questions with *wh-* question words. Then take turns asking and answering with a partner.

1. ___*Where*___ did you go on your last vacation?
2. _____ did you go? Was it in the summer?
3. _____ did you get there? By plane?
4. _____ did you do there?
5. _____ did you stay, one or two weeks?
6. _____ did you go with? Friends from work?
7. _____ did you go there?
8. _____ did it cost?

3   David is a movie director. Read the dialog and fill in the blanks with the present continuous of the verbs in parentheses. Then practice with a partner.

David: Jules, hi. Can I check my schedule for next week with you?

Asst: Of course. I've got your tickets, so ___*you're flying*___ (you/fly) to Cannes on Monday. _____ (1. you/arrive) at 2:30.

David: OK. What _____ (2. I/do) in the evening?

Asst: _____ (3. you/not do) anything in the evening.

David: Good. Now, on Tuesday _____ (4. I/watch) three movies.

Asst: No, that's Wednesday. On Tuesday _____ (5. you/meet) two American movie directors for lunch.

David: OK. What time _____ (6. they/show) my new movie on Thursday?

Asst: At 2:00 P.M.

David: OK. And when's the flight back?

Asst: _____ (7. you/come) back at 10:50 on Friday morning.

4   Cross out the word that doesn't fit in each group of words.

Ex: kindergarten   pre-school   ~~graduate~~

1. chemistry   career   physics
2. fine   yield   speed limit
3. part-time   junior   sophomore
4. instructor   professor   pedestrian
5. bachelor's   doctorate   PE
6. distance-learning   degree   online

Communication | make future plans
and appointments

5a ▶2.31 Listen to Ramon's phone call and answer the questions.

1. What is Ramon trying to schedule?

   _____

2. Why? _____

3. When is his appointment? _____

b Listen again and complete Jill's schedule for next week.

Jill

	Morning	Afternoon
Tuesday		
Wednesday		
Thursday	*teaching*	

c Read the How To box.

How To:

Schedule appointments	
Suggest a time	*Can you come on Thursday?*
Refuse politely	*I'm afraid I can't come then . . .*
Give reasons	*. . . because I'm working.*
Suggest alternatives	*I can come on Tuesday.* *How about earlier in the day?*
Make an appointment	*OK. let's meet at nine o'clock.*

6a **SPEAKING EXCHANGE** Work in pairs to schedule an appointment.

Student A: You are a college professor. Turn to page 130.

Student B: You are a college student. This is your schedule for next week. You can't change any of the things in your schedule. You want to see your professor (Student A) next week. Call him/her and make a one-hour appointment.

> *How about nine o'clock on Monday?*

> *I'm afraid I'm not available then.*

> *Are you free at eleven?*

b Check with another pair. Are your appointments for the same time?

	MONDAY	TUESDAY	WEDNESDAY	THURSDAY	FRIDAY
09:00			seminar from 9 to 11		
10:00	class from 10 to 12:45	class 10 to 12		take English test 10:30 to 12:30	
11:00					class 11 to 12:30
12:00		lunch with Emily 12 to 2			
1:00					
2:00					
3:00		play badminton 3 to 5	work in the biology lab all afternoon		doctor at 2:30
4:00					

Unit 11 Reference

can/can't

Use *can* to say that something is possible or to give permission. *Can't* is often used to explain rules.

> You **can't** drive through a red light.

Use *can* to ask about rules or ask for permission.

> **Can** we take photographs in the museum?
> Excuse me. **Can** I use your telephone?

have to/don't have to

	I/You/We/They	He/She/It
➕	have to	has to
➖	don't have to	doesn't have to
❓	Do . . . have to?	Does . . . have to?

Use *have to* to express an obligation—to say that something is necessary. Use it to explain rules.

> In Great Britain, you **have to** drive on the left.

Use *don't have to* when there is no obligation—to say that something isn't necessary.

> She's a member of the club, so she **doesn't have to** pay.

Note the difference between *can't* and *don't have to*.

> You **don't have to** wear a suit. (It isn't necessary, but you can wear one if you want to.)
> You **can't** wear jeans here. (It isn't allowed.)

Use *have to* to ask about rules.

> Do I **have to** get a visa?

Wh- questions

The common *wh-* question words in English are *what, who, when, where, how, which, whose,* and *why*.

A lot of questions are formed with *How* + adjective/adverb: *how much, how many, how long, how tall*.

Answer these questions with a number, price, quantity, etc.

> How much was your car? It was $20,000.

Note the answers to How long/tall/heavy/wide, etc.

> How tall are you? I'm six feet **tall**.
> How high is Mount Everest? It's about 29,000 feet **high**.

Present continuous for future

Use the present continuous to express future plans. Use it when the plans are certain; for example, when you have bought tickets/made arrangements/made a strong decision.

> We're meeting Sonia at the station at six tomorrow.
> John isn't starting his university course in October because he didn't pass his exams.

This tense is often used to ask about plans.

> What are you doing tomorrow evening?
> I'm having dinner with Yusuf. We're meeting in town.

Unit Vocabulary

Education

School subjects: history, chemistry, psychology, math, biology, geography, physics, literature, PE/physical education

Institutions: elementary school, college, kindergarten, pre-school, university/college, high school, middle school

Types of learning: classroom learning, adult education, online, part-time, distance learning

People: student, instructor, tutor, teacher, professor

Driving and road signs

Driving: test, driver's license, points, fine, traffic lights

Road signs: park, go, get gas, enter, pedestrians, yield, stop, speed limit, U-turn, turn left/turn right

UNIT 12
Your goals

A

B

C

D

Warm Up

1 Write captions for the photos, using words from Row 1 and one from Row 2.

Row 1	cycling	hiking	~~sailing~~	photographing nature
Row 2	desert	~~ocean~~	rainforest	savannah

Picture A:
sailing on the ocean

2 **Pair Work** Discuss.

1. Have you done any of the activities?

2. Did you like it or not? Why? Why not?

3. Do you want to try any of the activities in the future?

4. Do you think any of these activities are dangerous? Why?

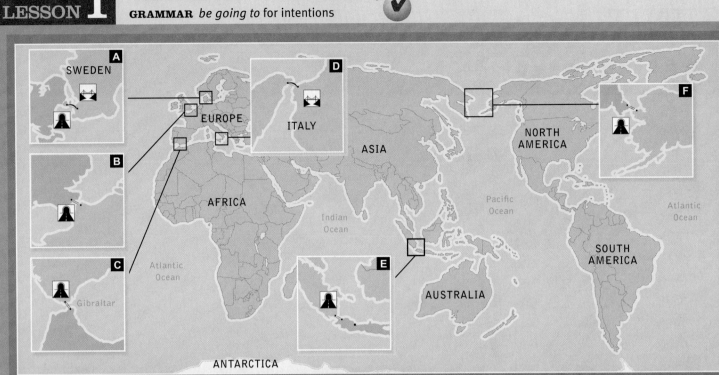

No more continents?

For centuries, natural barriers such as rivers, mountains, and seas have made travel difficult. Now, with modern technology, we are crossing these barriers and the world is becoming a much smaller place. Great Britain was an island for 8,000 years, but the Channel Tunnel opened in 1994 and connected Great Britain to mainland Europe. The Oresund Bridge and Tunnel opened in 2000 and connected Sweden to Denmark and the rest of Europe. Now there are more projects to link different parts of the world. The Italian government is going to build a 3-mile-long bridge between Sicily and the Italian mainland, and in Asia, Indonesia is going to build a tunnel between the islands of Java and Sumatra.

But there are bigger projects to join continents! Spain and Morocco are going to build a tunnel connecting Europe to Africa. They are thinking of building a 24-mile tunnel between Punta Palomas on the southern coast of Spain and Punta Malabata in northern Morocco, near Tangier. And the United States and Russia are discussing a project to connect Alaska to Siberia, joining the continents of North America and Asia.

Reading and Vocabulary | geography

1a **Pair Work** Look at the map. Answer the questions.

1. How many continents are there? What are they?

2. How do we travel between continents?

b Read the article and draw lines between the places that are or will be connected. Then match the places to A–F on the map.

_E_ 1. Java   a. the Italian mainland

____ 2. Sicily   b. Denmark

____ 3. Great Britain   c. Sumatra

____ 4. Alaska   d. mainland Europe

____ 5. Sweden   e. Morocco

____ 6. Spain   f. Siberia

c Look at the article again. Find and identify:

1. three verbs with the same meaning.

2. six words connected with geography.

Grammar | *be going to*

2   Complete the Active Grammar box.

<table>
<tr><td colspan="4">Active Grammar</td></tr>
<tr><td></td><td>I</td><td>We/You/They</td><td>He/She/It</td></tr>
<tr><td>➕</td><td>'m (am) going to + verb (base form)</td><td>_____ going to + verb</td><td>_____ going to + verb</td></tr>
<tr><td>➖</td><td>'m (am not) going to + verb</td><td>aren't (_____) going to + verb</td><td>isn't (_____) going to + verb</td></tr>
<tr><td>❓</td><td>Am I going to + verb?</td><td>_____ we/you/they going to + verb?</td><td>_____ he/she/it going to + verb?</td></tr>
</table>

See Reference page 126

3   Write sentences and questions about future plans with *be going to*.

Ex: Ford/build/a new electric car <u>Ford is going to build a new electric car.</u>

1. my parents/retire/next year _____
2. the Americans/build/a new space station/? _____
3. We/start/a new class/in September _____
4. I/not/take/a vacation/next summer _____
5. they/open/a new bridge/in 2020 _____
6. the city/not/build/any more airports _____

Pronunciation | word stress

4a ▶2.32 Listen. What do you notice about the pronunciation of *to*?

I'm going to stop smoking

b   ▶2.33 Listen and repeat these sentences. Then mark the stress.

1. She's going to lose weight.
2. They're going to sell their car.
3. We're going to learn French.
4. I'm going to buy a laptop.

5   **Pair Work** Ask and answer questions about your intentions with: *tonight, tomorrow, this weekend, on your next vacation.*

> *What are you going to do tomorrow?*   *I'm going out for lunch.*

Speaking

6   **SPEAKING EXCHANGE** Work in groups of four. Ask the students in your group questions.

Student A: Turn to page 130.   Student B: Turn to page 131.   Student C: Turn to page 132.
Student D: Find someone who is going to:

1. change their job soon.   2. write a novel before they retire.   3. have more than one child.

Write an informal letter

GRAMMAR infinitive of purpose

CAN DO ✓

Listening

1 ▶2.34 Listen to two friends talking, and answer the questions.

1. Where is Carol going? _____
2. Why is she going there? _____
3. Why does she want to study that? _____
4. What is she going to do in Cartagena? _____

Grammar | infinitive of purpose

2 Look at the <u>underlined</u> phrase in the Active Grammar box. Circle the correct letter to complete the rule.

> ### Active Grammar
>
> *And then I'll go down to Cartagena <u>to see the city</u>.*
>
> *To see* is an infinitive of purpose. The underlined phrase:
> a. gives instructions.
> b. explains the purpose or reason for doing something.

See Reference page 126

3 **Pair Work** Read the sentences aloud. Are the reasons true for you? If not, change them so they are true for you.

> **Ex:** I like to go on vacations to get a tan.

> *No, I like to go on vacations to see new places.*

1. I am studying English to get a better job.
2. I go to nightclubs to meet new people.
3. I go to work to have fun and relax.
4. I watch television to find out about other countries.
5. I listen to pop music to learn new information.

Speaking

4 **Pair Work** Imagine you are going abroad to study English. Think about your answers to the questions below. Then discuss with a partner.

1. Why are you going abroad to study?
2. Which country are you going to? Why?
3. Which city would you like to study in? Why?
4. Will you stay in a dorm, a hotel, or with a host family? Why?
5. What other places would you like to visit in the country? Why?

Reading

5 **Pair Work** Read the letter and discuss these questions.

1. How do we know that Vicky got a letter from Josie?
2. What comments does she make about Josie's message?
3. How do we know this is a letter between close friends?
4. Why does Vicky use exclamation marks (!)?

6 Read the How To box with expressions from the letter.

> Dear Josie,
>
> Thanks so much for your last letter. It was great to hear about your trip to Las Vegas. I was sorry to hear you lost so much money, but I'm glad you still had a really good time.
>
> Everything here is going fine. Everyone in my dorm is really cool, and there's a very cute guy on my floor! Most all of my classes are interesting, and there's one I really love—drama! I decided to take drama to get some more experience performing. And I'm getting a lot of chances to perform. We work with other students to present short scenes each week, and at the end of the semester we are going to perform a play. The instructor is excellent and a lot of the people in the class are very talented. Anyway, I'm really enjoying this semester!
>
> Write soon and say hi to Mom and Dad.
>
> Love,
> Vicky

How To:

Write an informal letter

Begin by mentioning the last letter you received	*Thanks so much for . . .*
Make a positive comment about it	*It was great to hear about . . .*
Describe your feelings	*I was so sorry to hear . . .*
Say something general about your life	*Everything here is going fine.*
End the letter	*Write soon and say hi . . .*

Writing

7 Write a letter to a close friend in another country. Use Vicky's letter as a model. Follow these steps.

1. Make notes about your life now.
2. Make notes about your future plans.
3. Organize your notes into paragraphs.
4. Write the letter.
5. Check the grammar and spelling.
6. Exchange letters with a partner. Help your partner correct mistakes.

Address: @ www.challengetravel.com

Adventure Travel

Wildlife Tours

Would you like to see the world's most magnificent animals in their natural habitats? Do you want to search for tigers in India, meet monkeys in Indonesia, or see polar bears near the North Pole?

Hiking and Trekking Tours

Whether you enjoy going on short, easy hikes or long, challenging treks, we have an adventure tour for you. Take a leisurely hike through the hills of Tuscany, or go on a once-in-a-lifetime 12-day trek to the Mount Everest base camp.

Cycling Tours

Would you enjoy taking a relaxing bike tour through the beautiful French countryside? Or are you an experienced mountain biker who wants to explore the volcanoes and rainforests of Costa Rica?

Contact us today.

Reading

1   Read the web page and answer the questions.

1. Where do you go to see polar bears? _____

2. Which hiking, trekking, or cycling tours are easier? _____

3. Which of the tours are more difficult? _____

4. Which tours do the photos show? _____

2   Look at the web page. Which adjectives match these definitions?

1. amazing and beautiful _____   3. done in a relaxed way _____

2. not easy to do _____   4. skill from doing something often _____

Listening

3a   ▶ 2·35 Listen. Nam and Tanya are looking at adventure tours. What tour do they choose? _____

b   Listen again and fill in the blanks with the correct form of the words in the box.

> can't stand   enjoy   like   want

1. They both _____ hiking.   3. They both _____ eating Italian food.

2. They _____ going on hard treks.   4. Nam _____ to see Italy.

Grammar | verb + infinitive/gerund

4 Complete the Active Grammar box with *to hike* or *hiking*. Then complete the rule.

Active Grammar

verb + infinitive (*to . . .*)	verb + gerund	verb + infinitive (*to . . .*) or gerund
want _____	*enjoy* _____	*love hiking or to hike*
would like _____	*can't stand* _____	*hate hiking or to hike*

Some verbs, such as *want* or _____, are followed by the infinitive (*to . . .*) form of a verb. Other verbs, such as _____ or _____, are followed by a verb and gerund. And some verbs, such as _____, or _____ can be followed by either the infinitive or gerund.

See Reference page 126

5 Fill in the blanks with the correct form of the verb in parentheses.

1. I enjoy _____ extreme sports. (do)
2. Bettina wants _____ an adventure cycling tour. (try)
3. We both love _____ animals in their natural habitat. (see)
4. Takao can't stand _____ on long flights. (go)
5. My friends would like _____ through Europe. (cycle)

Speaking

6 **Pair Work** Look at Adventure Travel's June tours below. Discuss which ones look interesting to you. Give reasons. Decide on one tour to go on.

Visit Machu Picchu.

Adventure Travel	June tours	
	Country	Level of difficulty
Great Wall of China Trek	China	challenging
Sahara Desert Hike	Morocco	challenging
Kilimanjaro Climb	Tanzania	extreme
Provence Cycle Tour	France	easy
Grand Canyon Trek	USA	challenging
Machu Picchu Hike	Peru	challenging
Great Barrier Reef Sailing	Australia	easy
North Pole Trek and Ski Tour	North Pole	extreme

7 **Group Work** Work with three or four other students. Discuss your travel goals. What's the most popular travel destination?

I really want to travel around Italy for a month.

Really? Me, too. I love Italian culture. What would you like to see and do in Italy?

Review

1 Here are some notes about a city's plans for next year. Use the notes to write five sentences with *be going to*. Begin sentences 1–2 with *They . . .* and sentences 3–5 with *The city*.

||||||||||||||||||||||||||||||||||||||||||||

- open a new bus station on Morton Road
- open a local history museum downtown
- close the swimming pool on Third Street
- introduce a lower speed limit downtown
- build a new bridge across the Logan River

Ex: *They are going to open a new bus station on Morton Road.*

1. _____

2. _____

3. *The city* _____

4. _____

5. _____

2 **Pair Work** Take turns using the cues to make either a negative statement [✗] or a question [?] using *be going to*.

Ex: Earth—get hotter [?] *Is the Earth going to get hotter?*

Ex: my sisters—visit us/next year [✗] *My sisters aren't going to visit us next year.*

1. the company—build a new factory [✗]
2. the situation—get better or get worse [?]
3. all the students—pass the examination [?]
4. my parents—sell their house [✗]
5. your father—retire/next year [?]
6. your team—win/next meet [✗]

3 Complete the sentences with *to* and the correct phrase from the box.

| pass the test | commute to work | send text messages |
| ~~get in shape~~ | meet new people | see the Acropolis |

Ex: I joined a gym *to get in shape*.

1. We went to Athens _____.
2. They are studying hard _____.
3. I'm going to join a club _____.
4. He uses his car _____.
5. Maria uses her cell phone _____.

4 Complete the sentences with the correct forms of the verbs in the box.

| become | marry | feel | fly | live | eat |
| ~~play~~ | smoke | study | travel | work | go |

Ex: Mandy loves *playing* tennis. She would like *to become* a professional.

1. I don't like _____, so I don't want _____ to college.
2. Pietro likes _____, and he would really like _____ around the world.
3. Josh enjoys _____ in restaurants, but he wouldn't like _____ in one.
4. Tanya can't stand _____, so she doesn't want _____ a smoker.
5. Harry hates _____ cold, so he wouldn't like _____ in a cold country.

Communication | plan study objectives

5 | Pair Work | Make a list of the ways to learn English in the photos. Do you do any of these?

6a What do you like about learning English? Complete Part 1 of the questionnaire below.

b | Pair Work | Discuss your answers.

7a What are you good at in English? Complete Part 2 of the questionnaire.

b | Group Work | Discuss your answers. Find other students who want to be better at the same things as you.

8a | Group Work | Work with the same group as in Exercise 7b. Think of ways that you can improve your English.

b Make a list of objectives for your group.

Our study objectives

We want to understand written English better, so:

1. we are going to use a monolingual dictionary.

2. we are going to read the same graded reader.

3. we are going to discuss the reader together.

Questionnaire
Part 1
Likes and dislikes in learning English

		I enjoy . . .	I don't like . . .
1	doing grammar exercises	☐	☐
2	learning new vocabulary	☐	☐
3	listening to English	☐	☐
4	listening to songs in English	☐	☐
5	reading English	☐	☐
6	doing pronunciation exercises	☐	☐
7	having discussions in English	☐	☐
8	doing roleplays and speaking games	☐	☐
9	writing in English	☐	☐
10	taking tests in English	☐	☐

Part 2
Strengths and weaknesses

		I'm good at . . .	I would like to be better at . . .
1	using English grammar	☐	☐
2	remembering new vocabulary	☐	☐
3	understanding spoken English	☐	☐
4	understanding songs in English	☐	☐
5	understanding written English	☐	☐
6	pronouncing English	☐	☐
7	expressing my opinion in English	☐	☐
8	doing things in English (like buy things)	☐	☐
9	writing English	☐	☐
10	taking tests in English	☐	☐

Unit 12 Reference

be going to

Form *be going to* with *be* and the base form of a main verb.

> **I'm going to take** my driving test next week.

	➕	➖	❓
I	*'m (am) going to*	*'m (am) not going to*	*Am I going to . . . ?*
We/ You/ They	*'re (are) going to*	*aren't (are not) going to*	*Are we/you/ they going to . . . ?*
He/ She/It	*'s (is) going to*	*isn't (is not) going to*	*Is he/she/ it going to . . . ?*

The contracted forms are usually used in spoken English.

> It**'s** going to be a cold winter.
> He **isn't** going to retire next year.

Use *be going to* to express a personal or impersonal intention (a strong wish to do something in the future).

Impersonal intention

> *Spain and Morocco* **are going to build** *a tunnel.*

Personal intention

> We**'re going to visit** Peru next summer.

Use the present continuous for fixed plans.

> They **are closing** the factory on February 24th.

Infinitive of purpose

Use *to* + infinitive to show the purpose or reason for an action.

> *I went to the store* **to buy some milk**.

(= I went to the store because I wanted to buy some milk.)

Verbs + infinitive/gerund

verb + infinitive (*to . . .*)	*want to go*
	would like to go
verb + gerund	*enjoy going*
	can't stand going
verb + infinitive (*to . . .*) or *gerund*	*love to go/love going*
	like to go/like going
	hate to go/hate going

Some verbs can be followed by an infinitive or a gerund.

> I **want to go** to the theater.
> I **enjoy going** to the theater.

Some verbs can be followed by either an infinitive or a gerund with no difference in meaning.

> I **like to go** to school.
> I **like going** to school.

Unit Vocabulary

Geographical/landscape features

bridge	canyon	continent	hill
coast	tunnel	mainland	sea
island	river	mountain	

Activities

cycling	horseback riding	mountain biking
sailing	mountain climbing	trekking
white-water rafting		

Adjectives: challenging   leisurely
extreme   magnificent   experienced

Speaking Exchange

Unit 1 | Page 13, Exercise 8

Student B

Ask and answer questions about these forms:

A: *Ok. Let's start with Form 1. Serena—what's her last name?*

B: *Perez—P-E-R-E-Z.*

A: *What's her nationality?*

1

First name:	
Last name:	P E R E Z
Age:	
Place of origin:	
Nationality:	M E X I C A N
Address:	
Email address:	s e r e n a . p @ e i c l . c o m
Telephone number (home):	
Telephone number (cell):	0 7 9 6 2 8 3 4 0 6 7
Occupation:	

2

First name:	C H A N G
Last name:	
Age:	2 7
Place of origin:	C H I N A
Nationality:	
Address:	8 4 W A L L S S T R E E T
	S Y D N E Y A U S T R A L I A
Email address:	
Telephone number (home):	0 2 9 2 3 4 5 7 0 1 0
Telephone number (mobile):	
Occupation:	A R T I S T

Unit 2 | Page 21, Exercise 7

Student A

Read the datebook on the right. Answer Student B's questions, then ask questions to complete your datebook.

Note: & = and

Unit 3 | Page 32, Exercise 4a

Student A

CALL 1 Answer the phone and start the conversation. (Jason isn't here today. Take a message for Jason.)

CALL 2 Your name is Chris. Call your partner. You want to speak to Sylvia. Your number is 202-555-0106.

Unit 4 | Page 42, Exercise 3b

Student A

Answer your partner's questions. Use this information:

Burger $3.95	Medium salad $4.00
Chicken salad sandwich $5.50	Large salad $4.95
Tuna salad sandwich $4.95	Regular coffee $1.95
	Large coffee $2.95
Ham and cheese sandwich $4.50	Small bottled water $2.25
Vegetarian pizza $5.95	Large bottled water $3.60
Pepperoni pizza $6.25	Orange juice $3.85
Regular fries $2.50	Regular soda $2.50
Large fries $3.00	Large soda $3.50
Small salad $3.45	

Rob Croft — Studio 2

8:00	get up & have breakfast
9:00	
9:15	open the studio
9:30	
10:00	meet clients & start recordings
1:00	
2:00	listen to the CDs from the morning & make changes
5:15	
5:30	finish work
5:45	
6:30	have dinner
7:00	
9:00	go to a nightclub with friends
11:30	

Unit 5 | Page 49, Exercise 7

Student B

Answer Student A's questions about this house.

For Sale

Three-story townhouse

- 2,000 square feet
- three bedrooms, two bathrooms
- living room, dining room, den
- large kitchen
- garage
- roof deck
- near center of town, close to schools, shops, and restaurants

$895,000

You are interested in a country house. Student A has the details. Ask questions to find out more about the house:

1. how big?
2. how many rooms?
3. what rooms?
4. garden/yard?
5. where?
6. price?

Do you want to buy the house?

Unit 5 | Page 55, Exercise 7a

Student A

You have this information from the Internet.

www.Furnishyourapartment.com

Bookshelves	**$50**
Lamp	**$45**
Large sofa	**$450**
Dining table and four chairs	**$395**
Armchair	**$125**
Large bed	**$250**
Coffee table	**$175**
CD player	**$100**
Today's special bargains:	
Television	only **$100**!!
Washing machine	only **$310**

Unit 6 | Page 61, Exercise 5a

Student A

Look at the pictures and cues. Tell your partner what happened.

Robin was outside the phone store. A woman on the other side of the street called for help . . .

woman/call for help

Robin/try to help   woman/escape
man/push/Robin into car

that night/men/push Robin/out of car
old man/watch them

Unit 7 | Page 75, Exercise 7a

Student A

Report one of the men missing and answer your partner's questions to describe him.

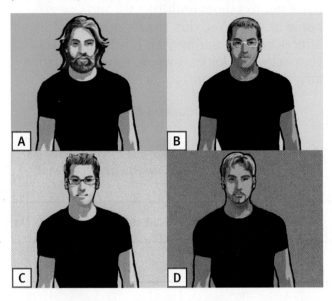

A   B
C   D

Unit 8 | Page 79, Exercise 7a

Student A

It is November. Next month you begin a three-month job in your company's office in Toronto, Canada. You don't know what clothes to take. Talk to a colleague, explain your situation, and ask for advice.

When you finish, give advice to your colleague (Student B). Remember it is very hot in Miami in the summer, but your offices have air conditioning and are quite cold.

Unit 8 | Page 81, Exercise 6

Student A

Ask and answer questions about the picture below. Write the missing names.

Unit 8 | Page 85, Exercise 8

Student B

Roleplay 1

You are a store clerk. You can't exchange the computer because you don't have another one in the store, but you can give refunds.

Roleplay 2

You bought a wool jacket for $150 last Wednesday. It doesn't fit. You want a refund or another jacket in a larger size.

Unit 9 | Page 91, Exercise 4b

Student B

| Casablanca | Hannibal Lecter | Cinématon |

Below are the answers to the quiz.

1. *Avatar* (2009)—it cost over $500 million.
2. *The Jazz Singer* (1928)—the first "talking film."
3. *Cinématon* (2009)—it's 150 hours.
4. *Shrek 2* (2004)—it made over $440 million in its first few months.
5. Harrison Ford—he's made over $300 million (*Star Wars, Raiders of the Lost Ark, Witness*).
6. Tatum O'Neal—she was ten when she won an Oscar for *Paper Moon* (1974).
7. *Casablanca* (1942)—with Humphrey Bogart and Ingrid Bergman.
8. *Psycho* (1960)—Alfred Hitchcock was the director.
9. Hannibal Lecter—Anthony Hopkins from *Silence of the Lambs* (1991).

Julianne   Pedro   Antonio   Kristin   Kim   Karina

Unit 10 | Page 99, Exercise 4

Student A

Ask your partners questions with *Have you ever . . . ?* If they answer *Yes*, find out when and where they did the activity, and if they liked it. Look up any words you don't know in a dictionary before you begin.

Have you ever been on . . .

- a cruise?
- a motorbike?
- a camel?
- a yacht?
- a jet ski
- television?

Unit 10 | Page 103, Exercise 6

Student A

You work for *Sunshine Travel*. Use this information.

Delta

Flights from JFK to Miami everyday. Cost $1280 per person round-trip for business class, $390 per person in economy. Flights stop in Atlanta for one hour.

US Airways

Flights from New York's JFK airport to Miami on Mondays, Fridays, and Saturdays only. Cost $253 per person round-trip in economy. Flights are direct to Miami.

American Airlines

Flights from JFK to Miami every day. Cost $1250 per person round-trip for business class, $453 per person in economy. Flights are direct to Miami.

Unit 10 | Page 105, Exercise 8b

Student B

Roleplay 1

You are the receptionist. Apologize and offer to give him or her a deluxe room with two double beds. (*I can give you . . .*). You start the roleplay.

Roleplay 2

You are the guest. You asked for breakfast at 7:00 A.M. in your room. It hasn't arrived and it's now 7:30. You have a meeting at 8:00. Call reception to complain.

Unit 11 | Page 115, Exercise 6a

Student A

You are Student B's professor. When he or she calls you, try to schedule an appointment. You don't get to school until 10 A.M., and you go home at 5 P.M. You don't see students before or after school, or during your lunch break. This is your schedule for next week. You can't change any of the things on your schedule.

> *How about ten o'clock on Wednesday?*

> *No, I'm afraid I'm not available then. Are you free at eleven?*

	MONDAY	TUESDAY	WEDNESDAY	THURSDAY	FRIDAY
9 A.M.					
10 A.M.	meeting 10 – 11:00	lecture from 10 – 12:30			
11 A.M.			staff meeting from 11 – 12:30		lecture 11 – 12:15
12 P.M.					
1 P.M.	lunch	lunch	lunch	lunch	lunch
2 P.M.	dentist 2:30	seminar 2 – 3:30		at conference all afternoon	
3 P.M.	lecture 3 – 5				seminar 3 – 4:30
4 P.M.					

Unit 12 | Page 119, Exercise 6

Student A

Talk to the students in your group. Ask them questions and find someone who is going to:

1. visit another country.
2. buy a new car.
3. go on a diet.

Unit 12 | Page 119, Exercise 6

Student B

Talk to the students in your group. Ask them questions and find someone who is going to:

1. join a club or team.
2. make lots of money in the future.
3. get married soon.

Unit 2 | Page 21, Exercise 7

Student B

Read the datebook below. Ask questions to complete it, and then answer Student A's questions.

Note: & = and

Rob Croft — Studio 2

8:00	
9:00	walk/take the bus to work
9:15	
9:30	make coffee & organize CDs for the day's work
10:00	
1:00	have a pizza/a sandwich at his desk
2:00	
5:15	clean the studio
5:30	
5:45	get home
6:30	
7:00	watch the news on TV/read the newspaper
9:00	
11:30	go to bed

Unit 5 | Page 55, Exercise 7a

Student B

You have this information from a catalog.

Ardent Catalog

Item	Price	Item	Price
Computer and printer	$400	Microwave	$60
Super vacuum cleaner	$99	Bed	$500
Coffee maker	$60	Bookshelves	$750
Desk	$99	Coffee table	$99
Large dining table and 6 chairs	$355	DVD player	$40
Small sofa with 2 armchairs	$325		

Unit 6 | Page 61, Exercise 5a

Student B

Look at the pictures and cues. Tell your partner what happened.

Robin was at the phone store and he decided to go home. He started running . . .

Robin/decide/go home   start/run home

Robin/halfway home   trip/bang head

After some time Robin/open eyes
decide/walk home   start/wrong direction

Unit 7 | Page 75, Exercise 7a

Student B

Report one of the women missing and answer your partner's questions to describe her.

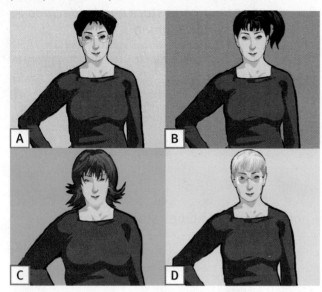

Unit 8 | Page 79, Exercise 7a

Student B

It is May. Next month you begin a three-month job in your company's office in Miami, Florida, USA. You don't know what clothes to take. Talk to a colleague, explain your situation and ask for advice.

When you finish, give advice to your colleague (Student A). Remember it is very cold in Toronto in the winter, but it is quite warm in your offices.

Unit 8 | Page 81, Exercise 6

Student B

Ask and answer questions about the picture below. Write the missing names.

Unit 9 | Page 91, Exercise 4b

Student C

The Jazz Singer	Harrison Ford	Avatar

Unit 10 | Page 99, Exercise 4

Student B

Ask your partners questions with *Have you ever . . . ?* If they answer *Yes*, find out when and where they did the activity, and if they liked it. Look up any words you don't know in a dictionary before you begin.

Have you ever been . . .

mountain climbing?	skiing?
horseback riding?	rollerblading?
skateboarding?	ice skating?

Unit 12 | Page 119, Exercise 6

Student C

Talk to the students in your group. Ask them questions and find someone who is going to:

1. join a gym.   3. move soon.
2. learn to play a musical instrument.

Writing Bank

Types of writing

1 Emails

- *Email* means "electronic mail."
- Email can be formal or informal.
- The text of an email does not include addresses or dates.
- Informal email often begins with *Hi* + name, not *Dear* + name. (the greeting)
- The opening sentence usually thanks the recipient (the person we are writing to) for their last email (or phone call or letter).
- The closing sentence usually mentions a future plan or wish (*I hope you can come./ Write soon.*).
- At the end of an email to a friend or a colleague, write *Best wishes,* + name. For a close friend or family member, write *Love,* + name.

2 Postcards

- Postcards are usually informal.
- Postcards are often sent by people on vacation, or to thank people for invitations, parties, and gifts.
- Begin postcards with *Hi* + name or *Dear* + name. (the greeting)
- The closing sentence usually mentions a wish or a future plan (*See you soon*).
- At the end, write *Love,* + name.

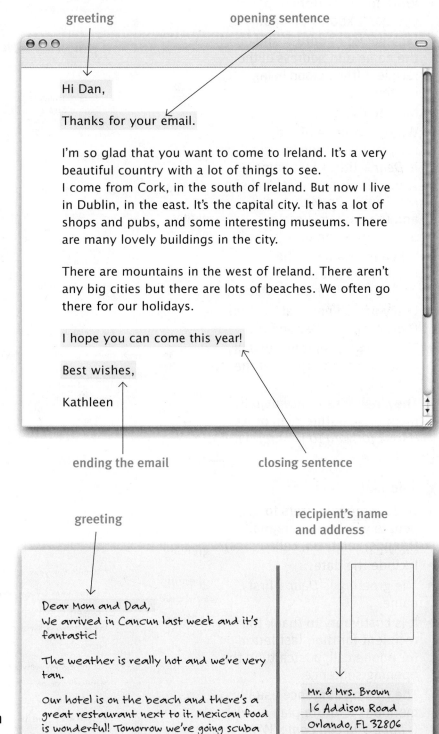

greeting

opening sentence

Hi Dan,

Thanks for your email.

I'm so glad that you want to come to Ireland. It's a very beautiful country with a lot of things to see.
I come from Cork, in the south of Ireland. But now I live in Dublin, in the east. It's the capital city. It has a lot of shops and pubs, and some interesting museums. There are many lovely buildings in the city.

There are mountains in the west of Ireland. There aren't any big cities but there are lots of beaches. We often go there for our holidays.

I hope you can come this year!

Best wishes,

Kathleen

ending the email

closing sentence

greeting

recipient's name and address

Dear Mom and Dad,
We arrived in Cancun last week and it's fantastic!

The weather is really hot and we're very tan.

Our hotel is on the beach and there's a great restaurant next to it. Mexican food is wonderful! Tomorrow we're going scuba diving and we're very excited.

Give our love to the children.

Love,

Donna and Andrew

Mr. & Mrs. Brown
16 Addison Road
Orlando, FL 32806
USA

ending

closing sentence

Writing Bank

③ Formal letters

- Write formal letters to people you don't know personally.
- Include your address and the name and address of the recipient (the person being written to).
- Include the date.
- When the name of the recipient is known the greeting is *Dear* + title + last name (*Dear Mr. Brown, Mrs. Jackson, Ms. López, Dr. Mahmud*) and the ending is often *Sincerely,* + name.
- When the name of the recipient is not known the greeting is *Dear Sir or Madam*.
- Use your full name at the end (*Jane Smith* or *Ms. Smith*).
- The opening sentence usually describes the purpose of the letter.
- The closing sentence usually mentions a future plan or wish (*I look forward to your reply*).

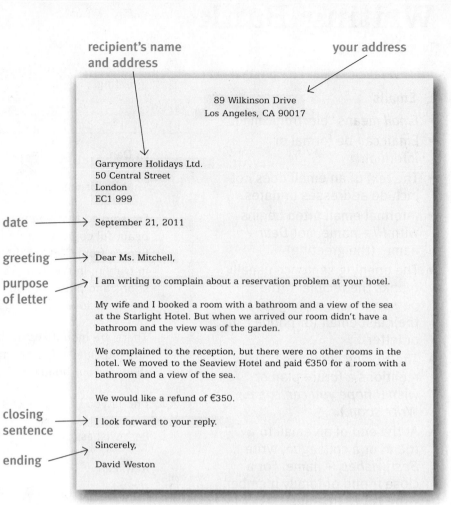

recipient's name and address

your address

89 Wilkinson Drive
Los Angeles, CA 90017

Garrymore Holidays Ltd.
50 Central Street
London
EC1 999

date → September 21, 2011

greeting → Dear Ms. Mitchell,

purpose of letter → I am writing to complain about a reservation problem at your hotel.

My wife and I booked a room with a bathroom and a view of the sea at the Starlight Hotel. But when we arrived our room didn't have a bathroom and the view was of the garden.

We complained to the reception, but there were no other rooms in the hotel. We moved to the Seaview Hotel and paid €350 for a room with a bathroom and a view of the sea.

We would like a refund of €350.

closing sentence → I look forward to your reply.

ending → Sincerely,

David Weston

④ Informal letters

- Write informal letters to people you know personally (friends, relatives, colleagues).
- Include the date.
- The greeting is *Dear* + first name.
- It is customary to thank the recipient for their last letter (or phone call/postcard) in the opening sentence.
- The closing sentence usually mentions a future plan or wish (*I hope you can come/Write to me soon*).
- At the end of a letter to a friend or colleague, write *Best wishes,* + name. For a close friend or family member, write *Love,* + name.

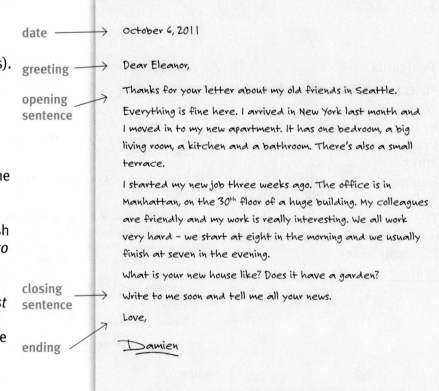

date → October 6, 2011

greeting → Dear Eleanor,

opening sentence → Thanks for your letter about my old friends in Seattle.

Everything is fine here. I arrived in New York last month and I moved in to my new apartment. It has one bedroom, a big living room, a kitchen and a bathroom. There's also a small terrace.

I started my new job three weeks ago. The office is in Manhattan, on the 30th floor of a huge building. My colleagues are friendly and my work is really interesting. We all work very hard – we start at eight in the morning and we usually finish at seven in the evening.

What is your new house like? Does it have a garden?

closing sentence → Write to me soon and tell me all your news.

Love,

ending → Damien

Pronunciation Bank

Consonants

Symbol	Key word	Symbol	Key word
d	**d**ate	ŋ	goi**ng**
b	**b**ed	s	**s**ofa
t	**t**en	z	**z**ero
p	**p**ark	ʃ	**sh**op
k	**c**ar	ʒ	televi**si**on
g	**g**ame	h	**h**at
tʃ	**ch**ild	m	**m**enu
dʒ	**j**ob	n	**n**ear
f	**f**our	l	**l**ike
v	**v**isit	r	**r**ide
θ	**th**ree	y	**y**oung
ð	**th**is	w	**w**ife

Vowels

Symbol	Key word	Symbol	Key word
i	b**e**	ə	**a**bout
ɪ	s**i**t	eɪ	d**ay**
ɛ	r**e**d	aɪ	b**y**
æ	c**a**t	aʊ	h**ou**se
ɑ	f**a**ther	ɔɪ	b**oy**
oʊ	b**oa**t	ɑr	c**ar**
ɔ	b**ough**t	ɔr	d**oor**
ʊ	b**oo**k	ʊr	t**our**
u	sh**oe**	ɪr	h**ere**
ʌ	b**u**t	ɛr	th**ere**
ɚ	w**or**d		

Sound	Spelling	Examples
/ɪ/	i	this listen
	y	gym typical
	ui	build guitar
	e	pretty
/i/	ee	green sleep
	ie	niece believe
	ea	read teacher
	e	these complete
	ey	key money
	ei	receipt receive
	i	police
/æ/	a	can man land
/ɑ/	a	pasta
	al	calm
	ea	heart
/ʌ/	u	fun sunny husband
	o	some mother month
	ou	cousin double young
/ɔ/	ou	bought
	au	daughter taught
	al	bald small always
	aw	draw jigsaw
/aɪ/	i	like time island
	y	dry shy cycle
	ie	fries die tie
	igh	light high right
	ei	height
	ey	eyes
	uy	buy
/ɛɪ/	a	lake hate shave
	ai	wait train straight
	ay	play say stay
	ey	they obey
	ei	eight weight
	ea	break
/oʊ/	o	home phone open
	ow	show throw own
	oa	coat road coast
	ol	cold told

Irregular Verbs

Verb	Simple Past	Past Participle
be	was/were	been
become	became	become
begin	began	begun
break	broke	broken
bring	brought	brought
build	built	built
buy	bought	bought
can	could	been able
catch	caught	caught
choose	chose	chosen
come	came	come
cost	cost	cost
dig	dug	dug
do	did	done
draw	drew	drawn
drink	drank	drunk
drive	drove	driven
eat	ate	eaten
fall	fell	fallen
feed	fed	fed
feel	felt	felt
find	found	found
fly	flew	flown
forget	forgot	forgotten
get	got	got
give	gave	given
go	went	gone/been
grow	grew	grown
have	had	had
hear	heard	heard
hold	held	held
hurt	hurt	hurt
keep	kept	kept
know	knew	known
lead	led	led

Verb	Simple Past	Past Participle
leave	left	left
let	let	let
lose	lost	lost
make	made	made
mean	meant	meant
meet	met	met
pay	paid	paid
put	put	put
read/rid/	read/red/	read/red/
ride	rode	ridden
ring	rang	rung
run	ran	run
say	said	said
see	saw	seen
sell	sold	sold
send	sent	sent
shine	shone	shone
show	showed	shown
sing	sang	sung
sit	sat	sat
sleep	slept	slept
speak	spoke	spoken
spend	spent	spent
stand	stood	stood
steal	stole	stolen
swim	swam	swum
take	took	taken
teach	taught	taught
tell	told	told
think	thought	thought
throw	threw	thrown
understand	understood	understood
wear	wore	worn
win	won	won
write	wrote	written

Audioscript

UNIT 1 Getting to know you

▶ 1.08 (Page 8)

Male: Where is Paulo Coelho from?
Female: He's from Brazil. He's Brazilian.
Male: Where is Hideki Matsui from?
Female: He's from Japan. He's Japanese.
Male: Where are Will Smith and Jada Pinkett from?
Female: They're from the United States. They're American.
Male: Where is Gerard Depardieu from?
Female: He's from France. He's French.
Male: Where is Penélope Cruz from?
Female: She's from Spain. She's Spanish.
Male: Where is Andrea Bocelli from?
Female: He's from Italy. He's Italian.
Male: Where are Ralf and Michael Schumacher from?
Female: They're from Germany. They're German.
Male: Where is Gael García Bernal from?
Female: He's from Mexico. He's Mexican.
Male: Where is Gong Li from?
Female: She's from China. She's Chinese.
Male: Where is Helen Mirren from?
Female: She's from Great Britain. She's British.
Male: Where is Nicole Kidman from?
Female: She's from Australia. She's Australian.

▶ 1.13 (Page 13)

Jake: Hi Yuko.
Yuko: Oh, hi, Jake.
Jake: Are you OK?
Yuko: No, I'm not . . . this is difficult.
Jake: What is it? Oh, I see. Look, I can help you.
Yuko: Thanks.
Jake: Your last name is your family name—Noda. And your first name is Yuko.
Yuko: OK. So, "age", what's that?
Jake: How old are you?
Yuko: Oh, OK. I'm 22.
Jake: Now, place of origin. Where are you from? Are you from China?
Yuko: No, I'm not from China, I'm from Japan.
Jake: And the city?
Yuko: Ah, yes, from Tokyo.
Jake: OK, so write Tokyo, Japan.
Yuko: T-O-K-Y-O, Japan. OK.
Jake: The next question, what's your nationality? That's Japanese. Right, and now, what's your address?
Yuko: 800 Park Avenue, New York, New York.
Jake: And what's your email address?
Yuko: It's yuko.noda@hotserve.com
Jake: And what about phones—what's your home phone number?
Yuko: 5-5-5-oh-1-2-6-5-8-9. This is easy.
Jake: And what's your cell phone number?
Yuko: 9-1-7-5-5-5-oh-1-5-2. Oh, what's this? Occupation?
Jake: Yes, what do you do?
Yuko: Ah, OK. I'm a student. Now . . . oh, that's all. Thanks very much, Jake.
Jake: That's OK. See you in class.
Yuko: Class? . . . Oh, yes! See you there.

▶ 1.14 (Page 15)

1
Female: Good morning.
Male: Hi.
Female: Are you a new student?
Male: Yes, I'm in the elementary class . . .

Female: Nice to meet you.
Male: You, too. Well, see you later.
Female: Bye.
2
Female: Excuse me.
Male: Yes?
Female: Are you our teacher?
Male: No, I'm a student in the . . .

Female: Great. Thanks for your help . . .
Male: OK. Bye.
Female: Goodbye.

UNIT 2 Work and leisure

▶ 1.17 (Page 18)

Interviewer: So, Jenny, you're a W Resort Club rep. Is it fun?
Jenny: Yes, of course.
Interviewer: Tell us about your typical day.
Jenny: OK. Well, I get up at about ten o'clock and go to the hotel around eleven. I meet the guests at a quarter past eleven and tell them about our parties and evening events, and I sell them tickets for excursions and day trips. Then I have lunch at about two o'clock.
Interviewer: Do you eat with the guests?
Jenny: No, I don't. I have lunch with the other reps.
Interviewer: And what do you do in the afternoon?
Jenny: At three thirty I go to the hotel pool and help with games.
Interviewer: Games?
Jenny: Yes, we organize all kinds of games and competitions for the guests. It's really fun.
Interviewer: Do you play the games?
Jenny: Oh no, I don't. I'm the referee.
Interviewer: So, what do you do in the evening? Do you have dinner with the guests?
Jenny: Yes, sometimes I do.
Interviewer: Where do you have dinner?
Jenny: I take the guests to a nice restaurant in town at a quarter to eight and then I take them to a nightclub at about ten thirty. Sometimes we have special parties and entertainment.
Interviewer: When do you finish work?
Jenny: Well, I leave the nightclub at about one thirty in the morning. So I get home at about a quarter to two.
Interviewer: What a busy life!
Jenny: Yes. But I love it!

▶ 1.22 (Page 22)

Male: You have a lot of interesting things for sale.
Female: Yes, we do. It's a two-family yard sale. Take a look around.
Male: How much is this book?
Female: It's a dollar fifty.
Male: Hmm . . . A dollar fifty?
Female: For you, I can sell it for a dollar.
Male: I'll take it. Here you go.

▶ 1.23 (Page 22)

Female: Hi. What are you looking for today? How about this laptop computer—it's old, but it works.
Male: Mmm. What about those watches?
Female: Yes, they're my daughter's watches. She likes lots of different colors.
Male: I see.
Female: And I want to sell these awful shoes, and the lamps—they are just terrible.
Male: Yes, they are.
Female: And I really want to sell this suitcase. Do you want to buy it?
Male: Uh, no, I don't think so.

▶ 1.24 (Page 22)

1
Female: What's this?
Male: It's a DVD player.
2
Female: What's that?
Male: It's a picture.
3
Female: What are these?
Male: They're cell phones.
4
Female: What are those?
Male: They're dishes.

▶ 1.27 (Page 23)

1
Security Officer: Excuse me, ma'am. Open your suitcase, please.
Female: Of course.
SO: What's this?
Female: It's a camera. It's for my son.
SO: And what are these?
Female: They're CDs. They're for my son, too.

2
SO: Open your bag, please, sir.
Male: OK.
SO: What's this?
Male: It's a laptop computer, for my work.
SO: Mmm. And what are these?
Male: They're magazines—computer magazines.
SO: And this?
Male: It's a scarf, for my wife.
3
SO: Open your purse, please.
Female: Oh, OK?
SO: What's this?
Female: It's my wallet, of course.
SO: And what's this?
Female: It's a datebook.
SO: Oh, what are these?
Female: They're scissors.
SO: I'm sorry, scissors aren't allowed in carry-on bags.

UNIT 3 Your free time

▶ 1.28 (Page 28)

Presenter: Traffic jams. We hate them, but what do we do in them? This is what some people say.

Carla: Traffic jams are OK. I think about work and plan my day. My daughter doesn't like traffic jams—she calls her friends, but I don't make phone calls in the car.

Gary: I shave and listen to the radio. I listen to the news. Unfortunately my car doesn't have a CD player.

Hiro: I don't do a lot, really. I hate traffic jams—they're so boring! I think about things or watch the people in the other cars. Sometimes I sing.

Lauren: We text or call friends on our cell phones.

Emily: Or we just talk. We don't usually listen to music.

▶ 1.29 (Page 29)

Journalist: Carlos, you're a very busy man, so I'm sure you use your lunch breaks. What do you do on your lunch break during the week?

Carlos: Well, you're right. I do a lot on my lunch breaks. I go for a walk or go swimming on Mondays and I go to the gym on Tuesdays. I sometimes meet friends on Wednesdays and we have lunch at a restaurant, and on Thursdays I sometimes listen to a lunchtime concert—when I don't have a lot of work to do. On Fridays I stay at my desk and work—I always have a lot of work to finish on Fridays.

Journalist: What about the weekend? What do you do on Saturday and Sunday?

Carlos: On Saturdays I go shopping—for food and also for other things, and on Sundays I relax. I sometimes watch soccer on TV and fall asleep.

▶ 1.31 (Page 32)

1

Tony: This is 555-898-4567. Please leave a message after the tone.

Jane: Hi Tony, It's Jane. Let's meet outside the theater at ten to eight. See you there, OK? Bye.

2

Sofia: Hello, this is Sofia and John's residence. We're not here right now so please leave a message with your name and number, and the time of your call. Thank you.

Steve: Sofia, it's Steve Henshaw here. It's three twenty on Wednesday. Can you call me? My number's 068-555-0752. Thanks.

3

Judy: Hi, I'm not here right now so please leave a message after the beep. Thanks.

Bill: Judy, it's Bill. Why don't we meet for dinner this evening? How about the Italian restaurant on Green Street at eight twenty-five? Give me a call. I'm in the office all afternoon.

4

Reception: Good morning. Brandon Travel Agency.

Mie: Hello. Can I speak to David Renton?

Reception: I'm afraid he isn't in this morning. Can I take a message?

Mie: Yes, can you ask him to call Mie Tamaka?

Reception: Of course. What's your telephone number?

Mie: It's 713-555-8834.

Reception: Sorry? Can you repeat that?

Mie: 713-555-8834.

Reception: OK, I'll give Mr. Renton the message.

Mie: Thanks. Bye.

▶ 1.32 (Page 32)

Female: Hello.

Male: Hi, can I speak to Laura, please?

Female: She isn't here right now. Can I take a message?

Male: Yes, please ask her to call Jeffrey.

Female: OK. What's your number?

Male: It's 555-908-5561.

Female: OK. Bye.

▶ 1.36 (Page 35)

Interviewer: David, how old are you?

David: I'm 22.

Interviewer: Do you have any special abilities?

David: Well, I can play the piano and the guitar.

Interviewer: Can you speak any foreign languages?

David: No, I can't. Only English.

Interviewer: Can you use computers at all?

David: Oh yes. I can use a lot of different programs. And I really like computer games. In fact I have a degree in computer programming.

Interviewer: Right. Well that's a useful degree.

David: Yes, but I don't like computer programming—it's boring.

Interviewer: OK. Can you drive?

David: Yes, I can.

UNIT 4 Food

▶ 1.38 (Page 40)

Lisa Redburn:

Hello and welcome to *In the garbage can*, the show where we look at people's lives by looking at their garbage. I'm Lisa Redburn. Today we look at the diets of two very different families. I have their garbage cans in the studio, with a typical day's garbage, so, let's start with garbage can A. What does this family eat and drink? We have some cans . . . soda cans—not very healthy. Mmm, instant coffee. Some boxes . . . cheese and tomato pizza, burgers. Some cookies, and . . . chips—all fast food, and not very healthy. Do they eat any vegetables or fruit? I don't think so. Gosh, not a healthy diet. A lot of this food is bad for you, so this family is probably not very healthy.

Now let's look at garbage can B. This is very different—it's good. This family eats a lot of fruit and vegetables . . . some potatoes, carrots, . . . bananas and apples. What do they drink? We have some cartons of juice, some milk cartons, and we have a water bottle . . . no two water bottles—very good, all very healthy so far. Tea bags . . . well, OK. They eat some pasta, and fish—that's good. I can't see any fast food here. I think this is a very healthy family.

▶ 1.41 (Page 42)

Server: Hi. What can I get you today?

Sam: Hi. I'd like a ham and cheese sandwich, please.

Server: On white or whole wheat?

Sam: On whole wheat, please.

Server: Would you like fries?

Sam: Yes.

Server: Regular or large size?

Sam: Large.

Server: And your friend?

Sam: Tracey, what would you like?

Tracey: Do you have salads?

Server: Sure. Small or large?

Tracey: Oh, I'd like a medium.

Server: OK. Anything to drink?

Tracey: Sam, do you want some juice?

Sam: No, thanks. Coffee for me.

Tracey: OK, a small cup of coffee for . . .

Sam: No, no, a large one.

Tracey: OK. A large cup of coffee for him, and a small bottled water for me.

Server: Fine. Coming right up.

Sam: How much is that?

Server: That's sixteen seventy, please.

Sam: Can I pay by credit card?

Server: Of course.

▶ 1.42 (Page 43)

1

Tracey: OK. A large cup of coffee for him and a small bottled water for me.

2

Sam: No, that's not for us.

3

Tracey: Vegetarian pizzas? I really like them.

4

Server: A medium salad for you?

5

Sam: Oh no, the salad's for her.

▶ 1.43 (Page 45)

Female 1: Hello. I'd like three bananas, six apples, and a melon, please.

Male: We don't have any melons today. Sorry.

Female 1: OK, just the bananas and apples, then, please.

Male: Six apples—that's two dollars, and three bananas—that's a dollar fifty. Here you are. That's three fifty, please.

Female 1: OK. Here's three and I have change . . . here's fifty cents.

Male: OK. Thank you. Bye.

Female 1: Hello. I'd like two pounds of ground beef, a pound of ground pork, and a whole chicken, please.

Female 2: Um, we don't have any chicken, I'm afraid.

Female 1: Oh well. OK.

Female 2: OK, so that's two pounds of ground beef, one pound of ground pork. That's fifteen dollars altogether. Thank you.

UNIT 5 Around the house

▶ 1.46 (Page 49)

Agent: The World of ResidenSea. Good afternoon. Can I help you?

Ryan: Yes. I'm interested in an apartment on the World of ResidenSea. Can I ask you some questions?

Agent: Yes, of course.

Ryan: Well, first of all. Are there any apartments for sale now?

Agent: Yes, there are, but we only have about three for sale right now. They're very popular.

Ryan: Yes, I'm sure. OK. How many bedrooms are there in the apartments?

Agent: Well, we have apartments with two bedrooms and apartments with three bedrooms. At the moment, we only have the two-bedroom apartments for sale.

Ryan: That's OK. I want two bedrooms, but how many bathrooms are there?

Agent: There are two bathrooms, one for each bedroom, and there's another toilet.

Ryan: Great, but how big are the apartments? I mean, how much space is there?

Agent: Oh, they're quite big. Some are 100 square meters and some are 120 square meters. The apartments for sale now are 100 square meters.

Ryan: That's good. OK, the big question . . . how much does the apartment cost?

Agent: The two-bedroom apartments for sale now cost around two million dollars.

Ryan: Two million dollars? Oh, I don't know about that. It's very expensive. Let me think about it for a day or two.

Agent: Yes, that's fine. Thank you for your call, and please call again. Goodbye.

▶ 1.47 (Page 50)

Amanda: So, where do you live, Pete? Do you have your own place?

Pete: Yes, I do. I have a studio apartment in the center of town.

Amanda: Does it have a yard?

Pete: No, it doesn't have a yard, but it has a small balcony.

Amanda: Is there a big kitchen in the apartment?

Pete: No, there isn't, but there's a kitchen area with a refrigerator, a stove, and a sink. I don't have a microwave.

Amanda: What about furniture?

Pete: I have a coffee table, and there are two chairs. And I have a beautiful sofa—I love that sofa, I use it all the time—I eat my meals there because I don't have a dining room table.

Amanda: Is there a TV?

Pete: Yes, of course. And I have a stereo.

Amanda: Do you have a computer?

Pete: Yes, I have a laptop—I use the Internet a lot.

Amanda: And do you have a cell phone?

Pete: Yes, I do.

▶ 1.51 (Page 52)

1

Teresa: My name's Teresa and I'm from Mexico. My favorite place in Mexico is Puerto Vallarta. It's a really popular beach town with many beautiful beaches. Puerto Vallarta is in the west, on the Pacific Ocean. It's a great place to swim, relax, and have fun.

2

Emilio: Hi, I'm Emilio. I love to hike in the Andes mountains. My best friend lives in Mendoza, Argentina. Mendoza is located just east of the Andes. It is a popular stop-over for hikers and skiers who are on their way to the mountains.

3

Luke: I'm Luke and I'm from the United States. One of my favorite places is Redwood National Park. It's in the northwest of California. It's an amazing forest filled with tall redwood trees. The trees are pretty old—in fact, a few are over two thousand years old.

4

Mee-Yon: Hi. My name's Mee-Yon, and I'm from South Korea. If you come to South Korea, visit Seoul. Seoul is in the north. It's a very modern and exciting city. There is a lot to see and do.

5

Ren: Hello. I'm Ren, and I live in Japan. One place in Japan I really love is Lake Biwa. Biwa is a very large lake in the center of Japan. It's not very far from Kyoto. It is a very old lake, and there are many fish and birds living in and around it.

UNIT 6 Around town

▶ 1.56 (Page 60)

Interviewer: What exactly happened yesterday, Mr. Andrews? Did you get lost?

Robin: I don't know. At about two thirty I walked downtown because I needed to get some money.

Interviewer: How far is the town from your home?

Robin: Not far . . . two miles. It's an easy walk.

Interviewer: Did you get the money?

Robin: Yes, I did . . . at the ATM in the bank, but I don't have the money now. Then I stopped by the phone store next to the bank . . .

Interviewer: Where did you go then?

Robin: Well, I wanted to go to a café but I don't remember . . .

Interviewer: What do you remember after that?

Robin: Well, I was in front of a library. I was on the ground. An old man helped me to get up. I was very tired . . . and I realized I was in Hartsdale.

Interviewer: Hartsdale is two miles from Scarsdale. Did you walk there?

Robin: I don't know, I really don't know.

Interviewer: Do you know Hartsdale well?

Robin: Not really. I was tired and lost. It was cold and dark. It was early morning, I think.

Interviewer: Did you have any money with you?

Robin: No, I didn't, not then.

Interviewer: So what did you do?

Robin: I asked the old man for directions to the police station. I tried to find it, but I got lost. I walked to the river and stayed under the bridge for an hour or two.

Interviewer: Did you go to sleep?

Robin: No, I didn't. I waited for the morning, then I walked back to the police station. They called my father, and he picked me up in the car.

Interviewer: So how do you feel now, Mr. Andrews?

Robin: I don't know . . . confused . . . it was all very strange.

▶ 1.57 (Page 61)

Robin: Listen . . . I can remember now. I know what happened. I stopped outside the phone store—I wanted to go in but there was a woman on the other side of the road. She called for help—there were two men there. I tried to help her and she escaped, but one of the men knocked me on the head with something and pushed me into a car. Then I don't remember anything—I was asleep, but I don't know how long, for how many hours. The men pushed me out of the car in Hartsdale, outside the library. There was an old man there. He watched and then he helped me.

▶ 1.58 (Page 61)

Female: Excuse me, do you know the way to the bus station?

Male: The bus station. Yes, it's easy. You turn left at the next street, Mill Street . . .

Female: Turn left, OK . . .

Male: Then go straight and you can see the post office on the corner.

Female: The post office.
Male: Yes, it's on the right.
Female: On the right, OK.
Male: At the post office, take a right onto Beech Road.
Female: Beech Road. OK.
Male: Go down one block, then turn left at the bookstore, onto Lime Avenue.
Female: OK.
Male: The bus station is on Lime Avenue. It's at the end of the street, on the left.
Female: OK, thanks very much.

▶ **1.59** **(Page 65)**

Customer 1: Excuse me, where can I find men's shoes?
Store guide: Men's shoes. They're on the third floor.
Customer 1: Thanks. Oh, and where are men's ties?
Store guide: Men's ties are in men's accessories, on the third floor too.
Customer 1: OK, thanks. Where are the escalators?
Store guide: The escalators are on your left.
Customer 1: Great. Thank you.

Store guide: Hi. Can I help you?
Customer 2: Yes, where are the kitchen knives?
Store guide: Ah, you want the housewares department. Housewares are on the lower level.
Customer 2: The lower level, OK. And can I find glassware there, too.
Store guide: No, glassware is on the fourth floor.
Customer 2: Fourth floor. OK, thanks.
Store guide: Certainly.

Store guide: Good afternoon. Can I help you?
Customer 3: Yes, thanks. I'm looking for a necklace, for a present.
Store guide: Jewelry is here on the first floor. Right over there.
Customer 3: Thanks. Oh, and where are your dining tables and chairs?
Store guide: They're in the furniture department on the fifth floor.
Customer 3: OK. Where are the elevators?
Store guide: Elevators are right next to the jewelry department.
Customer 3: Great. Um . . . Do you have a store directory?
Store guide: We certainly do. Here you go.
Customer 3: Thank you.

UNIT 7 Describing people

▶ **2.03** **(Page 70)**

Jane: Hello?
Mike: Hi Jane, it's me.
Jane: Oh, hello Mike. What's the problem?
Mike: You didn't write the names on those presents. Who are they for?
Jane: Sorry.
Mike: The electric drill. Is that for Alberto?
Jane: Yes, that's his.

Mike: And when's his birthday?
Jane: It's the third of next month.
Mike: What about the sneakers . . . are they David's?
Jane: Yes, the sneakers are his. His birthday's on the twentieth of this month.
Mike: What about the clock? Who is that for?
Jane: That's for Mr. and Mrs. Suzuki.
Mike: OK, so the clock is theirs. And the purse? Is that for Tara?
Jane: The purse? Of course not. That's mine!
Mike: It's yours? Oh. So what did you get for Tara? I know it's her birthday on the first of next month.
Jane: The datebook, that's hers.
Mike: Right. OK. Well, what about the umbrella?
Jane: The umbrella?
Mike: Yes, there's an umbrella on the table.
Jane: A black one?
Mike: Yes.
Jane: That belongs to us. It's ours!
Mike: It is? Oh yes. Of course . . .

▶ **2.07** **(Page 75)**

Scott: I want to report a missing person.
Officer: OK. Can I have your name first, sir?
Scott: Yes, it's Kennedy. Scott Kennedy.
Officer: Right. Thank you, Mr. Kennedy. When did you know this person was missing?
Scott: Yesterday evening. She didn't come back to the hotel.
Officer: When did you last see her?
Scott: Yesterday afternoon. We went to the museum together, then she went shopping.
Officer: OK. Let me complete this form. You last saw her yesterday afternoon, right?
Scott: That's right.
Officer: Your friend, what's her name and how old is she?
Scott: Um, Gemma, that's G-E-M-M-A, Gemma Hunston—H-U-N-S-T-O-N. She's 24.
Officer: Did you have an argument yesterday?
Scott: Oh no, you don't understand. She isn't my girlfriend. I met her a few days ago. She's just a friend.
Officer: I see. Well, maybe she decided to leave the hotel . . .
Scott: No . . . no. All her things are in her room.
Officer: OK. What does she look like?
Scott: Um . . . she's tall, about 6 feet. She has dark hair . . . dark brown . . .
Officer: Wait a minute . . . OK. How long is her hair?
Scott: Oh, it's not very long, and . . .
Officer: Hold on . . . What's her body type?
Scott: Excuse me?
Officer: Is she thin, heavy . . . ?
Scott: Oh, slim, she's very slim.
Officer: And what color eyes does she have?
Scott: She has green eyes, I think . . . yes, green.
Officer: And what's her skin color?

Scott: Well at the moment she's very tan.
Officer: Now, anything else. Are there any other features?
Scott: Oh, yes. She wears glasses. And she has a big bag with her, but it isn't hers. It's mine.
Officer: All right. And you last saw her yesterday afternoon. That's everything. Thank you, Mr. Kennedy. Can we call you at your hotel when . . .

UNIT 8 Dressing right

▶ **2.08** **(Page 80)**

Jools: Hello there, everyone, it's Jools and Anna here for today's round-up of the *We're watching you* house!
Anna: Yes, it's Day 4 in the *We're watching you* house, and things are changing!
Jools: That's right. Chloe left the house yesterday so now we've only got seven people here. Before we look at what happened today, let's see what they are doing now.
Anna: OK. Screen 1, the kitchen. Greg's in the kitchen—he's preparing dinner. He's cooking pasta, I think.
Jools: What's wrong with Greg? He's shouting about something.
Anna: Mmm, yes. Let's look at Screen 2—the girls' bedroom. Oh, that's Cara. Is she resting?
Jools: No, she isn't. Listen. She's crying. Maybe she had an argument with Greg.
Anna: Now, Screen 3, the garden. Jason's out there, but what's he doing? He's digging.
Jools: Yes, he's digging up the flowers. Look at his face—he's angry. Let's go to Screen 4—the gym.
Anna: OK. Yes, that's Erica—she's riding the exercise bike. Wow, she's cycling fast. And she's shouting . . .
Jools: No, she isn't shouting; listen, she's singing.
Anna: Well, I'm glad someone's happy! What's happening in the living room?
Jools: Screen 5 . . . Adam and Rosa . . . what are they doing? Are they talking?
Anna: Yes, they are, but they're talking very quietly. I can't hear them.
Jools: No . . . maybe they don't want the others to hear . . .
Anna: Or they don't want us to hear! Finally, Screen 6, the boys' bedroom. That's Gary . . . what's he doing?
Jools: He's looking for something . . . he's looking very carefully. What does he want? Oh, well. We can't watch him now. Let's look back at Day 4 . . .

▶ **2.10** **(Page 82)**

Forecaster:
Let's have a look at the weather map for Europe. Well, starting in the north, the weather isn't very good in Scandinavia—it's snowing in Sweden. It's foggy in the east of the UK, and at the moment it's raining heavily in the north of Germany. It's quite cold today in Poland—it's about five degrees in the east—and it's very cloudy in France. It's cloudy over the whole of France. The

weather is looking good in the south of Europe, though. As usual, it's very sunny in the south of Spain and it's warm in Greece—up to about 20 degrees today. Finally, be careful if you're driving in northern Italy—it's very windy. The wind is coming down off the mountains and it's very strong. That's it for today's weather in Europe, so let's look at . . .

▶ **2.11** **(Page 83)**

Female 1: Hi, how are you?
Female 2: I'm fine. It's a beautiful day, isn't it?
Female 1: Well, I don't know. I always get headaches when it's hot.
Female 2: Really? Maybe it's the sun.
Female 1: No, I don't think so. I think it's the temperature. My body doesn't like high temperatures.
Female 2: That's too bad. I always think the sun is good for people.
Female 1: Yes, you're right, but sometimes I feel very slow and heavy when it's hot. It's the temperature, not the sun. But it's so nice to see the sun.
Female 2: Oh yes, I agree.

▶ **2.12** **(Page 85)**

1
Customer: Excuse me. Can you help me?
Clerk: Certainly.
Customer: I bought this jacket yesterday and it doesn't fit.
Clerk: Do you want to try a different size?
Customer: No, I'd like a refund.
Clerk: Do you have your receipt?
Customer: Yes. Here it is.
Clerk: OK. So that's 150 dollars. Here you are.

2
Clerk: Can I help you?
Customer: Yes. I bought this DVD player last week and it doesn't work.
Clerk: I see. Do you have your receipt?
Customer: Yes, I do. Can I exchange it for another one?
Clerk: Of course. Just a moment. Here it is.
Customer: Thanks very much.

UNIT 9 Entertainment

▶ **2.13** **(Page 89)**

1
I usually read the news on the Internet because it's free. My newspaper costs about a dollar a day, but it doesn't cost anything to read the news on the Internet, so the Internet is cheaper than newspapers for me.

2
I use news apps on my cell phone to find out about sports results—I get the results almost as soon as they happen, but on the TV you need to wait for the next news show. Apps are faster than TV.

3
I like immediate news so I use the Internet or watch TV. You get complete news stories on the Internet, but on TV you get only a few facts about the news story, so the Internet is more detailed than TV.

4
I'm very busy and I don't have time to read newspapers, so I always watch the evening news on TV. Anyway, watching the news on the TV is more exciting than reading newspapers because it's visual.

5
I know it sounds old-fashioned, but I love the radio, and that's where I get my news. The radio is easier than reading newspapers or watching TV because you can listen when you're doing other things.

6
I don't like reading so I watch TV or listen to the radio to get the news. I think that TV is better than the radio because it's more interesting—you can understand things more when you see pictures.

▶ **2.15** **(Page 90)**

Host: Good evening. The actor Trey Summers is here to talk with us about movies. [applause] Hi Trey.
Trey: Hi Laurie.
Host: So what are your favorite movies of the last ten years, Trey?
Trey: That's a hard question. But, you know, I think the *Pirates of the Caribbean* movies are my favorite. They are certainly the most exciting movies of the last ten years. Johnny Depp is always great. And I think the stories are the most interesting.
Host: What's your favorite comedy?
Trey: That's an easy one. *Shrek*. I love all the *Shrek* movies. I think they are the funniest movies. And yes, they are the best animated movies I know of.
Host: What do you think the most unusual film of the last ten years is?
Trey: The most unusual? I'd have to say *Alice in Wonderland*. Now that was creative. And the story and costumes were very strange—it was one of the strangest movies, I think.
Host: And what about the scariest movie of the last ten years?
Trey: That's a hard one. You know, I actually think *The Dark Knight* was the scariest. It was the most violent movie, for sure. And the Joker, man was he scary. Heath Ledger was great in that part.

▶ **2.16** **(Page 92)**

Jessie: Look at this wonderful photograph. It shows Central Park in New York City. Christo put up big gates and covered them with orange cloth.
Frank: Well, that's different . . .
Jessie: What do you think about this one? The shark in the tank? It's by Damien Hirst. He's the most popular living artist these days.
Frank: Hey, that's a real shark! That's just strange. Why did Hirst make that? What does it mean?
Jessie: I don't know. I think it's about life and death. I think it's very interesting.

Frank: I like traditional art better than contemporary art. Look at this painting of the bedroom. That's my kind of art. It's beautiful.
Jessie: That's by Vincent Van Gogh. Do you like Impressionist paintings?
Frank: Well, I guess I like Impressionist paintings better than sharks.
Jessie: What do you think about this sculpture?
Frank: That huge animal? Is it a dog?
Jessie: Yes! It's by Fernando Botero. It's called *Dog*. Don't you just love it?
Frank: Well, I guess it's kind of interesting.
Jessie: What about this painting by Roy Lichtenstein? I really love Pop art.
Frank: It looks like a comic book. You call that art?
Jessie: Yes, I do. I think it's wonderful.
Frank: Which do you like better, the Van Gogh or the Lichtenstein?
Jessie: Hmm . . . I think the Lichtenstein.
Frank: I really don't understand . . . In any case, I think I like sightseeing better than looking at art. Why don't we go see Central Park?

▶ **2.17** **(Page 93)**

Frank: There are so many things to do in New York. What do you want to do tomorrow? Any ideas?
Jessie: I'm not sure. I'll get the guidebook. Um. What about the Empire State Building?
Frank: That sounds good.
Jessie: OK. Let's go to the Empire State Building in the morning. Now what about the afternoon?
Frank: I'd like to see Times Square. Is that nearby?
Jessie: I'll look at the map. Yeah, it's pretty close.
Frank: OK. We'll go there after lunch then.

▶ **2.18** **(Page 95)**

Male: So, Saturday. Any ideas?
Female 1: How about a movie?
Male: During the day?
Female 1: Yes.
Female 2: I don't like watching movies during the day, really.
Female 1: OK. Well, why don't we go to the pool? We can go swimming.
Male: There are always lots of children in the pool on Saturdays.
Female 2: And I don't like swimming very much.
Female 1: Well, how about going shopping then?
Female 2: Yeah, I like shopping better than swimming.
Male: There's that cool mall in West Hollywood . . .
Female 1: That sounds like fun.
Male: What about the stores on Rodeo Drive?
Female 2: No, the stores are more expensive there.
Female 1: Yes, and Beverly Hills is very crowded on Saturdays.
Male: All right, we'll go to West Hollywood then.
Female 2: I think the mall in West Hollywood has a good Japanese restaurant.

Female 1:	Well, let's go to the mall in the morning and then we can have lunch there.
Female 2:	OK, that sounds good.
Male:	Let's meet at eleven.
Female 1:	OK. We'll meet at eleven outside the main entrance.

UNIT 10 Going places

▶ 2.19 (Page 98)

Evan:	I'm here at Chicago's O'Hare Airport with the Garfield family: Derek and Moira and their children Todd and Alicia. Today's the start of an amazing adventure for them. In half an hour they get on a plane to begin the vacation of a lifetime. Derek, how are you feeling right now?
Derek:	To be honest, Evan, I'm feeling pretty nervous . . . nervous but excited.
Evan:	Why are you nervous?
Derek:	Well, this is my first long plane trip. I've never been on a really long flight before. So it's my first time . . . and Australia is a long way away.
Evan:	Are the rest of you experienced world travelers?
Alicia:	We've been to Mexico!
Moira:	Yes, the three of us have been on a long flight before. I took Todd and Alicia to Mexico City last year.
Evan:	Have you ever been to Australia?
Moira:	No, we haven't.
Derek, Alicia, Todd:	No, we've never been to Australia.
Alicia:	I'm looking forward to going horseback riding, hiking, and bungee jumping!
Evan:	Have you ever been horseback riding, hiking, or bungee jumping before?
Todd:	Alicia and I have been horseback riding. We went horseback riding when we were in Montana two years ago. But mom and dad stayed in the hotel. They've never been on a horse.
Moira:	It was cold.
Derek:	But we've all been hiking. We went last year.
Evan:	And have you ever been bungee jumping?
Derek:	Oh no. We haven't been bungee jumping. It's the first time for all of us.
Moira:	I'm very nervous about it.

▶ 2.22 (Page 103)

Agent:	Good morning. Hawaii Discount Travel.
Mika:	Hi. Do you sell discount air tickets to Maui?
Agent:	Yes, we do.
Mika:	Great. I'm interested in four tickets from Honolulu to Maui.
Agent:	What's your destination on Maui? Do you want to fly into Kahalui? We have more flights to that airport.
Mika:	OK, Kahalui is fine.
Agent:	All right. And what day do you want to travel?

Mika:	We'd like to leave this Friday.
Agent:	One-way or round-trip?
Mika:	Round-trip, please. We'd like to come back on Monday.
Agent:	OK. Let me check . . . Do you want economy or business class?
Mika:	Economy, please.
Agent:	And what time do you want to depart?
Mika:	In the early afternoon.
Agent:	Let me see. Four round-trip tickets leaving this Friday afternoon. OK, The best prices are on Island Air and Hawaiian. On Island Air it's a hundred and forty-four per round-trip. Hawaiian is a little more — it's a hundred and eighty-two.
Mika:	I think I'd like the cheaper one, Island Air. Are there any stops?
Agent:	No, it's a direct flight.
Mika:	Great. What time does the flight leave?
Agent:	At one thirty, arriving at two-twenty. And the return flight departs at two-ten and arrives in Honolulu at three.
Mika:	OK, I'd like four tickets, please. What's the total?
Agent:	That'll be five seventy-six total.

▶ 2.23 (Page 105)

Reception:	River Oaks Hotel. Can I help you?
Female:	Yes. I'd like to reserve a room, please.
Reception:	Certainly. What's your date of arrival?
Female:	May 15th.
Reception:	For how many nights?
Female:	For two nights. May 15th and 16th.
Reception:	We have standard and deluxe rooms available on those nights.
Female:	How much are the standard rooms?
Reception:	Standard rooms are one sixty-nine per night and deluxe rooms are one ninety-nine.
Female:	OK. I'd like a standard room with two double beds.
Reception:	Alright.
Female:	And do you have a spa?
Reception:	Yes, we do.
Female:	I'd like to reserve a spa treatment, too, then.
Reception:	Yes, I can arrange that. But first may I have your name and credit card number?

▶ 2.24 (Page 105)

1

Reception:	Can I help you?
Male:	Yes. I asked for a room with a king-sized bed.
Reception:	Yes.
Male:	Well, you've given us a room with two single beds.
Reception:	Oh, I am sorry, sir.
Male:	Can we have a room with a king-sized bed, please?
Reception:	Let me see . . . yes, we have one on the second floor.

2

Reception:	Reception. Can I help you?
Woman:	Yes, I ordered tea with my breakfast.
Reception:	Yes?
Woman:	And they've given me coffee.
Reception:	I'm so sorry. I'll call the kitchen and get you some tea right away.
Woman:	OK. Thank you.

UNIT 11 Education

▶ 2.25 (Page 109)

Foreign visitors coming to the United States usually have to have an International Driver's License. An International Driver's License translates details of your driver's license into English and other languages. You can get an International Driver's License in your home country.

If want to rent a car in the United States, you usually have to have a credit card. At some rental car agencies, you can use a debit card, but the company will take a deposit from your account. At most rental car companies, you have to be 21 years old to rent a car. And if you are under 25, you usually have to pay an extra fee.

▶ 2.26 (Page 109)

Brian:
We don't have a lot of rules in the United States really. I mean we don't have to do military service and we don't have to have identity cards. You can drive when you're 16 and you can even buy a gun when you're 21. But some things aren't so easy. You have to be 21 to go into a nightclub, and smoking is difficult — you can't smoke in offices, stores, or restaurants. And of course we have to pay when we see a doctor or go to hospital.

▶ 2.27 (Page 110)

Interviewer:	Nicole, tell us about the educational system in New Zealand. For example, how long do students spend in the system?
Nicole:	Oh, . . . a long time. Usually about 17 or 18 years if they go to university.
Interviewer:	When did you start school?
Nicole:	At the age of five. Compulsory education is twelve years — from five to about sixteen, but a lot of children in New Zealand go to pre-school classes, you know, kindergartens. I went to a kindergarten when I was four and after a year I went to primary school.
Interviewer:	How many years were you at primary school?
Nicole:	Five years — from five to ten.
Interviewer:	Where did you go after primary school?
Nicole:	Well, then I went to an intermediate school, from ten to twelve. Then at twelve we start at secondary school.
Interviewer:	Mmm. When can students leave secondary school?

Nicole: Well, we can leave secondary school at sixteen, but most students stay till they're eighteen.

Interviewer: Do a lot of students go on to higher education?

Nicole: Yes, I think about fifty per cent of students go into higher education—that's universities, polytechnics, colleges of education . . .

Interviewer: Which type of institution did you go to?

Nicole: I went to a college of education because I wanted to be a teacher. I became a primary teacher, so I studied for three years and finished when I was twenty-two.

Interviewer: Do you have to pay for your higher education studies in New Zealand?

Nicole: Yes, we have to pay some of the costs, but not all.

Interviewer: How much does a student have to pay?

Nicole: Oh, it depends. It can be 2,000 dollars or it can be 20,000.

Interviewer: Well, thank you, Nicole. That was very interesting . . .

▶ **2.30** **(Page 113)**

Host: Interested in taking an interesting class, maybe even getting a college degree? Today we'll be talking to three people who can help you do that. First is John Wells of Open University. Hi John. Can you tell us about the school?

John: Yes, Open University offers online classes so students can study at home and get a college degree.

Host: How much do classes cost, and how long do they last?

John: Classes cost four hundred dollars and they take five weeks to complete. Our students can get a college degree in just two years.

Host: What degrees do you offer?

John: You can get a degree in almost any area—art, biology, history . . .

Host: Great! And now let's talk to Meg Morgan from the French Cooking Institute. Hi Meg. Tell us about the institute.

Meg: Well, we're the number one French cooking school in the city, and besides courses for professional chefs, we offer a variety of short classes that are open to everyone.

Host: What kind of classes?

Meg: Well, two of our most popular classes are chocolate making . . .

Host: Mmmm.

Meg: Yes! And the art of making French bread.

Host: Wonderful! Where do students study?

Meg: All classes are at the institute in our large, fully-equipped kitchens.

Host: How much does a class cost?

Meg: Classes are six hundred and fifty. That's for twelve hours of instruction. And all of our instructors are top chefs.

Host: Thanks, Meg. And now let's talk to Ted Lopez. Tell us about your company, The Learning Attic.

Ted: Well, we're number one in adult education in America. We offer a wide variety of classes for adults.

Host: What are some of your most popular classes?

Ted: We have so many . . . "Speak Spanish in one hour" is very, very popular. Also, of course, "Get rich quick." But really, people love so many of our classes.

Host: Where do students take the classes?

Ted: Both online and in classrooms all over the US.

Host: How long are classes and much do they cost?

Ted: Most of our classes are two to three hours long, and most cost just forty-five dollars.

Host: Interesting! We'll find out more after this short break.

▶ **2.31** **(Page 115)**

Alders: Hello. Jill Alders.

Diaz: Mrs. Alders? It's Ramon Diaz. My son, Mateo, is in your class.

Alders: Oh yes, Mr. Diaz. How can I help you?

Diaz: I'd like to meet you next week to talk about Mateo's grades.

Alders: All right. Can you come on Thursday? I'm teaching in the morning, but I'm free in the afternoon.

Diaz: I'm afraid I can't come then because I'm working. What about Wednesday?

Alders: I'm afraid I'm teaching all day on Wednesday.

Diaz: Well, I can come on Tuesday.

Alders: Um, Tuesday. Well, I'm teaching a class at ten thirty and I'm taking the children swimming in the afternoon.

Diaz: How about earlier in the morning?

Alders: Let me see . . . OK. Let's meet at nine o'clock.

Diaz: Nine o'clock on Tuesday morning. Thank you very much.

Alders: I'll see you next week then.

UNIT 12 Your goals

▶ **2.34** **(Page 120)**

Mark: Why do you have this guidebook for Colombia?

Carol: Oh, didn't I tell you? I'm going there next month.

Mark: You're going to Colombia?

Carol: Yeah, to study Spanish.

Mark: Wow, sounds exciting. I didn't know you wanted to study Spanish.

Carol: Yeah, I want to study Spanish to make my work a bit easier. I go to South America sometimes for work. A lot of people speak English, but I want to be able to speak some Spanish, too.

Mark: Why not study Spanish in Costa Rica or Mexico? Why in Colombia?

Carol: To learn Colombian Spanish. Everybody says it's a beautiful accent.

Mark: I didn't know that. How long are you going to be there?

Carol: Well the course lasts three weeks, but I'm going to stay an extra week to do some sightseeing.

Mark: Oh really?

Carol: Yes, my classes are in Bogotá, which is great. It's a big, busy city with a lot of things to see and do. I'm going to stay with a Colombian host family—that way I'll speak Spanish outside of class too. And when my classes are over, I'll go down to Cartagena to see the city. It's supposed to be beautiful. And to go swimming. It's on the Caribbean and I hear the beaches are wonderful.

Mark: Sounds great. I'm jealous!

Carol: Well . . . Why don't you come with me?

▶ **2.35** **(Page 122)**

Nam: This agency has a lot of adventure hiking tours. Do you like hiking?

Tanya: Yeah, sure, I enjoy hiking . . .

Nam: Me, too. Being out in nature and seeing wildlife . . .

Tanya: But I can't stand going on really long, hard treks. You get so tired and dirty.

Nam: Yeah, I guess I feel the same. I did the Grand Canyon trek and it was hard. Hmm . . . This sounds interesting . . . Hike in the Sahara Desert. What about that? I love to visit extreme places.

Tanya: The Sahara? Don't you think that will be a little hot? I hate hiking in really hot weather.

Nam: Yeah, that might be a problem. Well, what about hiking in Europe? Here's one . . . Hike in the Italian Alps.

Tanya: Yeah, that sounds cool. And I like eating Italian food!

Nam: Me, too. And I want to see Italy— I've never been there. And maybe we can go to Switzerland or France, too.

Tanya: OK, I guess I'd like to do the Italian Alps hike.

Nam: Well, let's see how much it costs. Europe can be expensive.